Property
PROFITS

Joan!

I hope you enjoy my book. Here's to your future successes in real estate.

PROPERTY PROFITS

A Lazy Investor's Guide to Making Money in Real Estate Even if You Don't Have Time or Patience for All the B.S.

Carlos A. Rodrigues

BRIGHTFLAME
Books By Experts

BRIGHTFLAME BOOKS, TORONTO

First Edition. Published in Canada by BrightFlame Books, Burlington, Ontario. www.BrightFlameBooks.com

Table of Contents

Limit of Liability/
Disclaimer of Warranty

Dedication

Wow, where do I start? There are so many people that deserve special mention.

To my wife Sharon who followed me down the real estate investment rabbit hole even when she wasn't sure it would work out, to my mother who always offered words of encouragement when the chips were down, to my kids Allegra and Armando who still think the houses I work on are so cool, to my many friends, family and mentors, thank you. You have all been a special part of my success...

But this one is for you Pop. I would not be where I am today without You. You showed me what it takes. No guts no glory! And when there is no help in sight and you feel like the pressure is going to squash you...you find a way to suck it up and power through.

Introduction

What Does Real Estate Have to Do with Retirement?

If you're holding this book, there's a good chance it's because you're not completely thrilled with the progress of your retirement plan. Maybe you've been watching the ups and downs of the market, wondering if you've missed the opportunity to make your move. Maybe you've been concerned at seeing those ups and downs reflected in your investment portfolio. Maybe you've become frustrated with the assurances of your broker, who says that mutual funds are the only thing that will give you a decent rate of return.

Or maybe, instead, you picked up this book because it said "real estate" on the cover, and you want to know more. Most of us know someone, even if it's just a friend of a friend, who has done very well for himself or herself by investing in real estate. If you're like most people, the idea of owning and renting out property seems like a simple, straightforward way to make money. But then you second-guess yourself. Even if you have the cash to buy a new home just sitting around, you don't have the time or interest in doing all the work it takes to get rich from real estate. Yes, you want to build your wealth, but you're not the "tycoon" type.

I've been a real estate investment consultant since 2007, and in that time, no one has come to me with hopes of owning entire residential blocks or developing a neighborhood from the ground up. In fact, most people who come to me aren't thinking about real estate at all. They're thinking about an alternative to the same old-same old investment approach. They're tired of putting away a big chunk of their income every month without seeing the progress they were led to expect. They've been denying themselves for years, saying "no" to unplanned expenses and sticking to their budget, all in the hopes of creating a secure future for themselves. But when they look at their quarterly statement, they're feeling the opposite of security. They feel frustrated, confused, maybe even scared.

It shouldn't be that way.

When you work hard, you deserve to feel rewarded. That goes double for people who work hard and save hard. If you're putting aside money for retirement each month, but not seeing the rewards, maybe it's time for a new approach to investment.

What We Think About, When We Think About Investment

Investment is more than a matter of making money—it's also about making the best use of your time. After all, you only have so many years for your money to work for you behind the scenes before you need to pull it out and start living off it.

Moreover, the money you've saved is never static. Inflation dictates that if your money isn't making more money, it's losing value.

So, if the return on your investment isn't at least a percentage point or two greater than the average rate of inflation, you're losing money *and* wasting time.

Wealth isn't just about what's in your bank account. It's what you can do with what's in your bank account. And the fact is that nobody, even your most trusted advisor, is going to take care of what's in your bank account like you are.

That's another common complaint I hear from people who are fed up with the traditional approach to investing. Not only are they not seeing the progress they want, but they feel frustrated by the lack of control they have over their portfolio.

If you've ever complained to your financial advisor about this, they'll likely tell you that the rule with mutual funds is to be steady and consistent, and the fluctuating market is an opportunity to be taken advantage of. The market is always going to fluctuate, but if you have a consistent contribution, the number of units purchased when the market is down will be greater, given that the cost per unit is lower. At that point, you'll be buying more units in that mutual fund than you would when it's consistently moving up. That, they'll tell you, is the benefit of "dollar cost averaging."

From a mathematical standpoint, they're right. The problem is that mutual funds bring the risk of reverse dollar cost averaging as well. In other words, even the steadiest contribution to your investment accounts can't guarantee the value of those accounts when you go to make a steady monthly withdrawal. After all, the funds you're buying into don't stop fluctuate each month because you're ready to start drawing from those accounts. The value of your investments could be far below what you expected.

For mutual funds to really pay off, you have to minimize the effect of the ups and downs of the market upon withdrawal. That means being constantly aware of what the market is doing. And let's be honest: who wants to spend their retirement micromanaging their mutual funds? Wouldn't it be easier to have a steady stream of income that comes in reliably every month, remains under your control, and requires minimal maintenance? And let's not forget the biggest benefit: never worrying about what effect your withdrawal is having on your overall investment.

That's exactly what you get when you invest in real estate.

Rather than working with conceptual units assigned an arbitrary value from one day to the next, investing in real estate means working with a hard asset, something that fulfills a basic human need. You're not forced to cross your fingers and hope for the best from the market. Even in years when the market increase of real estate in your area is flat, you're still able to make a profit from your investment.

What "Your Money" Really Means

The rule of thumb around retirement saving is to put away 10 percent of what you make. However, that amount is simply not an option for most people. For most middle-class families, it's a stretch to put away even $100 a month. And what those people don't realize is that a good portion of their money stops being their money once they invest it into a mutual fund.

To begin with, there are hidden costs of doing business in a mutual fund. In Canada the average equity mutual fund takes 2.35 percent out of your investment every year for management purposes, regardless of whether or not you make money. That is a ton of money being siphoned out of your contribution—money that never goes to work for you. Add in inflation and taxes, and your retirement savings are considerably less than the amount you're contributing each month.

Again, the bank advisors will tell you that it's not about a quick return—it's about slowly and steadily building up your money over time. But that slow, steady build up doesn't always happen the way you expect.

Let's say you put $100,000 in your mutual fund portfolio on day one, and in a year's time, the value has increased to $120,000. You think, "Great! I made $20,000—things are going well with my money." But that's only your money if you liquidated your account that day. Six months later, the value of your investments could easily drop several thousand dollars. The value is likely to go up and down, over and over, as the years proceed. What happens if the time when you need that money coincides with a bad time in the market?

If you're a mutual fund investor who is ready to retire, it's only natural to feel outrage when you realize that your accounts are not ready for you to quit working. You feel that you've been lied to. But the reality is that nobody lied. They simply didn't tell you that there is a better way.

So, What's the Difference with Real Estate?

Let's start with the obvious.

Unlike traditional investments, real estate involves a physical asset. It's not just a piece of paper—it's something that provides concrete, material value in the real world. Even if the housing market fluctuates wildly and your home loses 10 percent of its market value, that doesn't mean that 10 percent of your house is gone. It's still there, putting money in your pocket each month. As a physical asset, real estate gives you far more control over your investment.

Another difference is revenue streams. Where traditional investment brings in revenue from just one or two sources—the performance of your stocks in the market or possibly the effect of a different currency—real estate investment draws in not one, not two, but four different streams of revenue.

Stream 1: Positive Cashflow

This is the rental income left over after all your monthly expenses on the property (mortgage, insurance, taxes, maintenance, etc.) are paid.

Stream 2: Market Value Increase

All things being equal, in the US and Canada, the government is committed to keeping a steady rate of annual inflation. With that inflation rate comes an automatic increase in your property's value.

Stream 3: Mortgage Paydown

Every month, as you put a portion of your rental income into paying off your mortgage on the property, you own a little more equity in that property. Depending on how you choose to access that equity, the money generated can be a tax-free boost every so often.

Stream 4: Claiming Depreciation

In Canada, we can claim asset depreciation on our taxes, even when the fair market value goes up. This revenue stream relates to saving money on your taxes, not to actual income. However, in the end, it's all money in your pocket.

With four streams of revenue from a single asset, it's not surprising that people of average income are making amazing leaps in their ability to generate wealth.

A few years back, I began working with Jim, a client whose income was $50,000—slightly below the middle-class average. After saving for years but not seeing his retirement fund go up by much, he took the plunge into real estate and bought three single-family homes as rental properties. After about five years, he and I sat down to discuss the progress of his investment. We totaled up the four streams of revenue from each of his properties.

If he'd gone the traditional route and put away 10 percent of his $50,000 annual income, he'd have saved up about $25,000 during those five years.

Instead, he'd put away $600,000, as much as if his salary had been $1.2 million a year for those five years.

Moreover, each of those properties was on track to be worth close to $1 million by the time he planned to retire.

For a man who had worked hard all his life and denied himself many luxuries for the sake of future security, this was an incredible moment. No, he hadn't made a killing that allowed him to quit his job then and there. But what he did have was a robust head start on the path to a secure future. If he held onto those properties until he reached retirement, he would have a $4 million nest egg waiting for him. He could either sell the properties and cash in, or he could continue renting them at a gradual increase to match the rate of inflation (or more, if the neighborhood were to get hot), and continue enjoying a fantastic return on his investment.

I tell this story to just about everyone who comes to me skeptical of real estate investment. I know that it can be intimidating to enter unfamiliar financial territory, but all it really takes to understand is a good look at the numbers. Ask yourself whether you'd rather fight your way to making $70,000 a year but struggle to put 10 percent away, or make $50,000 a year and never have to put a dime away because your investments are doing it for you.

Need a minute to think about it?

Your Life Is Waiting

I remember reading a Forbes article that said 87 percent of the world's workforce hates what they do. That number is burned into my brain. Just imagine it...

87 percent of people hear their alarm go off and feel a sense of dread at the day that awaits them.

87 percent of people spend all day doing something that they have no sense of passion for.

87 percent of people hate their lives from Monday to Friday.

Now consider a second statistic: 80 percent of people work until age 65. Put those two together, and you'll realize that the majority of people are going to be doing something they hate right up until a few years before they die. If they're lucky, they'll have up to 15 years to live life on their own terms. But only if they've been able to put away at least 10 percent of their income each month. If they've only been able to put away $100 or so per month, their final years are going to be almost as miserable as their working life was.

That's why I get so excited about sharing the good news about real estate investment. To me, real estate represents a light at the end of the tunnel. It certainly was that for me.

Investing in real estate allowed me to exit a job I didn't enjoy and achieve true lifestyle freedom. Thanks to my investment properties, my time is now my own. If I want to take an entire day off to spend time with my family, or just waste an afternoon by taking my kids out for ice cream, or go on a European vacation for a month or two, I can. More importantly, I'm able to live my life without pinching pennies or worrying about my family's future.

For me, real estate investment has become a way of life. But it doesn't have to be that for everybody. You might love your career and have no desire to leave it. However, you're probably still looking forward to a time when you don't *have* to work anymore. For you, real estate investment can provide the peace of mind you crave, allowing you to enjoy your day-to-day life without that nagging anxiety about your future security.

You might also be one of that large majority of people who aren't engaged by their jobs. Maybe the only thing that keeps you going to work each day is that you're too close to retirement to start over now. If that's you, real estate investment offers an opportunity to get up each morning with a greater sense of purpose. When you see your savings multiplying at a significant rate—not just 3 or 5 percent, but 30 percent or more—it's a lot easier to feel like your hard work is going toward something truly productive.

And who knows? At a certain point, you might find yourself in a position where you can walk out of the uninspiring job forever. Where you no longer have to say "Yes, sir" every time your boss tasks you with extra grunt work. Where you don't have to come into the office early or on weekends anymore, or sit around in pointless meetings, or go on business trips that take you away from your family.

That was how my life looked for years. I'd be out at client appointments and receive text messages from my wife, telling me about the cute and sometimes incredible things our kids had done. Even today, it chokes me up to remember that I missed seeing my son take his first steps, because I was away at work. Knowing that I was doing it for my family didn't lessen the pain of missing that priceless moment.

That's what makes this approach to investment truly life-changing. It's about so much more than money—it's about never having to miss those important life moments again.

It's also about being present for my life in a whole new way. Knowing that the bills are going to get paid, no matter what, has removed that nagging voice of anxiety about the future, the one that eats away at so many of us without our even realizing it's there.

For years, there was an invisible elephant sitting on my chest and I never realized it. All of a sudden, I could breathe. And being able to breathe was the first step in a whole new way of life. No longer treading water, but moving forward.

Real estate investment hasn't made me a billionaire or an influential person in my community. Nevertheless, it has made me feel tremendously powerful. Why? Because money is no longer a deciding factor in what I do or how I spend my time. It's hard to fully express how liberating that feels—you just have to experience it for yourself.

Taking That First Step

I know what you're probably asking yourself right now.

"If real estate investment is as profitable as he's making it out to be, why doesn't everyone do it?"

The answer is simple: investing in your first property is a big step. You go from having one mortgage to two. For most people who aren't already extremely wealthy, taking that step seems unfathomable.

Moreover, once you've purchased the property, you're paying for maintenance—electricity, heating, insurance—while possibly waiting weeks, or even months, to find the right tenant. (Those initial weeks of suspense often lead people to make bad decisions about renters, which turn into the horror stories you might have heard from other property owners.)

There's no question that the first few months of investing in your first property can bring challenges. But if you have expert guidance, those challenges are surprisingly easy to overcome.

That's what this book is all about—helping you take those first steps safely and successfully. My goal is to guide first-time real estate investors through my proven process for making money through buying and renting out property. I'll show you different ways to go about setting up your rental system—few people realize that there are multiple approaches to real estate investment, one to fit every temperament and long-term profit goal. I'll also coach you past the pitfalls so that you don't become a victim of your own impatience.

Like every big change, there's a learning curve involved. But I've packed this book with strategies, tips and stories from my time as a real estate investor as well as a financial advisor to ensure that your investment pays off, both financially and in terms of your peace of mind.

You can spend your whole life putting away a big share of your income, only to find your retirement fund coming up short of what you need to maintain your lifestyle. You can overinvest in the wrong stocks or sell at the wrong time, and watch in horror as your nest egg is decimated. But in real estate investment, the biggest mistake you can make is letting fear of the unknown keep you from taking action.

This book will walk you step-by-step through setting up a successful, sustainable property investment on your own. However, there's an even easier approach to launching your property portfolio–one that requires no research, legwork or maintenance on your end.

If you'd like to cut to the chase and learn about this simple, proven approach to real estate investment, put down this book, pick up your phone or tablet, and visit **www.LetsTalkRealEstate.today**

There's a great quote from the movie *After Earth* that I always share with first-time clients:

> *"The only place that fear can exist is in our thoughts of the future. It is a product of our imagination causing us to fear things that do not at present and may not ever exists. This is mere insanity. Don't misunderstand me. Danger is very real, but fear is a choice."*

Yes, there will be bumps in the road, problems to solve, choices to make. But ultimately, wouldn't you rather be the one to make those choices than leave them up to a bank advisor with a one-size-fits-all mentality about investment? By getting expert advice, weighing the options yourself, and picking the one that makes most sense for your goals, you get to be in control of your money. You don't have to trust someone else with your future. You can take control of it yourself.

So, what does real estate have to do with retirement?

As it turns out, everything.

Chapter 1

Why Do I Invest in Real Estate? (It's More Than Money)

Years ago, I was working at a financial planning firm when John walked into my office. I'd met him before—he owned the duplex next to my grandparents' home, and we'd struck up a conversation across our front porches. He had a warm smile, a bone-crushing handshake, and an infectious enthusiasm, especially about world travel. When I mentioned that my family came from Portugal and I'd been there several times, he surprised me by knowing even more about the country than I did.

Since the last time we spoke, John's mother had passed away, leaving him a life insurance policy that she'd purchased when he was born. That's when I realized that John was the person my firm had been trying to get in touch with for the past several weeks. We had handled his mother's estate and were responsible for letting him know that the policy was available to him, but we had had no luck reaching him since his mother's death.

After discussing the details of his policy, John and I got to talking, and the conversation eventually turned to the topic of investments. This wasn't an accident—John's policy left him a lot of easily accessible cash, and as a financial planner, it was naturally my job to sell him on the investment opportunities we could handle for him. Since the insurance policy earned hardly any interest, I suggested that we move his cash into something that would potentially work harder for him. Something like mutual funds, or segregated funds—things we advised our clients on and that I myself had personally invested in.

In response to my advice, John said the words that would change my life.

"I only invest in real estate," he told me.

A Mind-Blowing Story

John told me that he started buying properties when he was still working as a principal in elementary school. By the time he retired, he had 65 properties to his name, which he'd held onto in the ten years since retiring. He wasn't bashful about sharing that real estate had made his life pretty amazing, both while he was working and especially now.

Aside from the minimal time he spent maintaining his properties, he traveled the world practically nonstop. That's what made him so difficult to get in touch with, he said, especially because he rarely planned any of his vacations. Instead, he and his wife would go to the airport and, in his words, "see what's on tap." Did they want to go somewhere warm? Did they want to visit family? Did they want to experience someplace new? Whatever sounded good at the time, they would walk up to the desk, buy tickets, and away they'd go.

As you can imagine, everything about this blew my mind. The idea of dropping into the airport and flying anywhere on a whim sounded like a dream life to me. I couldn't believe that this guy, a former elementary school principal—as far from a "tycoon" as you can get—was living that kind of life. The kind of life I'd been dreaming about for ages.

Some people daydream about wealth, or status. But my ongoing daydream was about a life where my time was my own. I didn't mind working, but I hated being tied to a 9-to-5. I wanted to be able to wake up on a beautiful morning and spend hours over coffee with my wife or take my kids to the beach to build sandcastles. I wanted to fit work in around the important stuff in life, instead of the other way around.

I'd always assumed this type of life was reserved for the elite or the incredibly wealthy. The fact that John was living this way expanded my ideas of what was possible for regular people like us. But even more mind-blowing was the fact that he'd created this life through real estate investment.

As a kid, I'd watched my dad buy, maintain and manage rental properties for a number of years. He liked working on the homes, and I liked helping him. As a result, real estate had always been something that, in the back of my mind, I wanted to venture into one day. But for some reason, my dad always tried to talk me out of it. It never made sense to me why he was against my investing in real estate, though I knew it must have something to do with the fact that he'd sold off all his properties years before. I figured there must be some hidden cost, some downside that I'd never noticed.

But the way John told it, there was no downside. Real estate investing had given him the freedom to live out the retirement of someone with fifty times his net worth.

Finally Free

In the weeks after that meeting, I couldn't get John's story out of my head. What I'd seen my father do was clearly not the full picture of real estate investment. I saw it as more of a second job that helped financially sustain our family. I never got the sense that buying and managing property was a way to improve your lifestyle.

Given the hard work I'd put in alongside my father, the idea of having more than 60 properties was almost unfathomable to me. But John was proof of what real estate investment at that level of strategy could do for someone.

The more I thought about it, the more sense it made. Compared to financial management, buying and maintaining properties involved a lot fewer variables. Investing in real estate was like growing a tree. It took some effort at the outset to plant and establish, but once the tree was mature, all I had to do was visit it once in a while to keep it healthy.

I purchased my first property in 2009. It was on the east end of the Hamilton Mountain, one of the more desirable neighborhoods in the area where I live. Even with all the advantages of the property, I almost didn't buy it, because it had an oil furnace—I didn't want to be bothered with filling the tank every six months, not to mention the financial and environmental problems that would be unleashed if the tank ever deteriorated and leaked. But my real estate agent at the time said, "If you're not going to buy it, do you mind if I do?" Looking back, her words could have been a clever ploy to get me over the second-guessing stage. If it was a ploy, it worked—I used the equity from my family home as a down payment to take out a mortgage on the property, signed the papers, and *voila*! I was a landlord.

Right off the bat, my confidence in this new venture was tested. The house needed a lot of basic updates before it was ready for the type of tenant I wanted. Leaky roofs needed to be fixed, an overgrown tree needed to be cut down, and of course there was that outdated furnace to be replaced. I could do some of the work myself, but not all of it. I was scared out of my mind—with the new mortgage and the cost of repairs, I was now on the hook for an extra $1200 per month. What if it didn't work out? What if my investment didn't pay off?

> Nowadays, I laugh to think how scared I was at that amount, knowing all the ways that the "worst case scenario" can be reworked to an investor's advantage. But at the time it was a significant amount for us, and I'd never done this before.

With all that in the back of my mind, I was absolutely shell-shocked when the time came to do my taxes. Even with all the expenses it required to buy and update, my property investment had yielded a profit of $300 per month. All our bills were getting paid, with no anxious rejigging of our budget and no credit card debt hanging over us. On top of that, we were able to go on not one, but two vacations that year. Never in my wildest dreams would I have guessed that such a small amount of income, coming in steadily every month, could change our lives so dramatically.

And that was just the change we were seeing. Taking into account all the four income streams I set out above, we had put away an extra $29,000 that year. For us, at that stage in our lives, that was serious money. And the fact that I'd done hardly any extra work to earn it? It's hard to explain that feeling. I walked around town feeling as though I'd stumbled onto a treasure chest buried in my backyard. It was exhilarating—I felt completely free; as though anything I wanted was possible.

Maybe it's just how my mind works, but I instantly began to imagine about how much more could be out there. Not just for me, but also for my financial management clients. These were people who, just like me, lived as small as possible while working as hard as possible, in order to have a secure future. They worried about paying the bills every month, hoping that no big unexpected expenses would jump out and ambush them. Now that I knew what a huge change could come from so little effort, I wanted them to know about it, too.

Real-Life Success Stories

In 2013, I launched the real estate arm of my financial services firm, Magellan Wealth Management. My goal was to make real estate investment simple and accessible for people who were ready to use their money to make a tangible, immediate difference in their quality of life.

In the years since then, I've seen that John's story is far from being an anomaly.

- Steve, the former president of North America's largest telecommunications supply company, decided one day that he was ready to retire. He purchased a couple properties to make up the income that he lost from his job. Today he's able to dedicate his time to following his passion for physical and spiritual self-improvement, travel, and any other business ventures that come his way.

- Evelyn, a 20-year-old McMaster University student whose parents moved to London, Ontario rented out her family home to fellow students. By the time she graduated four years later, she'd not only paid off her tuition in full, but had the expertise to add four more properties to her portfolio. Today, eight years later, she has ten properties, and a steady stream of income that allowed her husband to retire at age 30.

- Mike, a long-time constable with Toronto's police force, invested in real estate as a strategy to build his retirement fund. (As you might guess, his law enforcement experience made him a natural property manager.) At just 40 years old, he's well on the way to retiring from the police and living off the yield of his investments.

- Andrew got started in real estate investment at age 22, intending to buy just one or two properties. But when he saw the power of what it could do for him, he went all in. Today, ten years later, he owns ten investment properties around the world. In addition to having a portfolio worth over $3 million, he's currently building 40 townhomes, and coaches others in how to invest in real estate.

Walking alongside people as they watch their lives change in front of them is the most rewarding part of my job as an investment consultant. I live for the moments when a client opens their first cheque and I see the look on their face that says, "I wasn't expecting it to be *this* good."

You're in Control of Your Money

There are a lot of assumptions people make about real estate investment. The most common assumption is that the process is just like those shows on HGTV where the hosts turn a dilapidated old wreck of a home into a glossy single-family palace with up-to-the-minute appliances and décor.

While it's fun to watch these transformations on TV, most people aren't interested in taking on a giant renovation project like that, even if it means making a ton of money in the end. (And by the way, it usually doesn't.)

Personally, I enjoy working on the rental properties I own. Not only do I have a passion for real estate, but it takes me back to childhood memories of swinging a hammer alongside my father. As a result, I can happily spend one weekend after another renovating one of my properties until it looks just how I want it to.

However, if you're not someone who has that expertise or passion, it certainly doesn't mean that real estate investment isn't for you. While most of my clients enjoy seeing the properties they've purchased, few of them are interested in doing the day-to-day work of renovation or management. They don't want a second job. They simply want a reliable way to make their money work for them.

That's just one more advantage of real estate investment over mutual funds and other, more traditional forms of investment. Depending on your personality, your long-term goals, and your budget/time preferences, there are several different ways for you to approach real estate investment. (We'll go into more detail about these different approaches in the next chapter.)

But whether you enjoy getting involved in the nitty-gritty or prefer to sit back and wait for your check to arrive in the mail, real estate investment is the rare type of investment that gives you full control over your money. You don't have to hope that a broker does the right thing with your money, or that the value of your investments holds steady until you're ready to retire. Whether you're buying the property yourself or lending the money as a joint venture partner, *you* get to make the decisions about where your money goes and what it's doing for you.

The Benefits Outweigh the Challenges

I wouldn't be a responsible consultant if I told people that there are no risks in real estate investment. Like any other form of investing, there are challenges and unique problems to work through. (We'll go over these potential challenges in Chapter 4, along with the easy ways to deal with them.)

However, in my view, those problems are a drop in the ocean compared to the vast benefits that real estate investment offers. Among those benefits are a remarkably consistent rate of return, and an easy capability for recession-proofing your investment. But for me, the main benefit of real estate investing is the freedom it offers for living your life on your own terms.

As a financial planner, my day was tied to my desk. I couldn't do my job unless I was spending most of my day face-to-face with clients. But as a real estate investor, I can do just about everything from the comfort of my own home…or, for that matter, from a seat on a plane that's about to take my family and me to a European island for three months. (Yes, that's actually happened.)

While real estate investment does involve its share of problem solving, the problems are not as difficult as you might think. Real estate investment is that rare method of earning income where the money you make doesn't have to own you.

A Great Substitute for a Pension

Back when I was a full-time financial planner, people would come to me and confess their fears about not having enough money to live comfortably once they retired. I don't mind saying that I put together some great financial plans for people— sometimes even I was impressed with what I managed to pull off in terms of the money they'd have in the end…*if* they followed the plan.

That, of course, was the big question. All the financial plans I created required a certain amount of lifestyle change. Just about anyone could retire with any amount they wanted, if they were willing to discipline their spending habits in the short term. But in nine out of ten cases, I knew that the financial plans I'd created would end up abandoned in a desk drawer. People got their plans back from me and balked at even the smallest changes required of them. It was a brutal experience sometimes.

All I could do was remind them that they had come to me for advice. "You're asking me to give you the steps it will take to change your life for the better," I'd say. "I can show you how to hit your goals, get out of debt, and make sure you can maintain your current lifestyle once you finish working. But that's all I can do. Making it happen is up to you."

Sometimes people are simply stubborn, unwilling to give up little luxuries in exchange for something greater. But there are also people for whom even scraping together an extra $100 per month to put into a retirement fund would mean eating cat food for meals.

I can relate to both sides. Even though I used to be a financial planner by profession, in my personal life I can't save worth a damn. (Go figure, right?) And only a few years ago, putting aside $100 per month was not remotely possible for me. Real estate investment was what shifted the balance of my financial situation, making it easy to put aside money each month. (I'll share more about this story in Chapter 5.)

That's another reason why I'm so passionate about sharing real estate investment with people. If everyone just had one rental property and held onto it until retirement, no one would ever have problems maintaining their lifestyle after they quit working. Once that rental property is paid off, it will put $2,000-$3,000 a month in your pocket. If you ask me, that's a pretty great substitute for a pension.

More importantly, real estate investment doesn't require waiting until you retire to live the life you want. My own family is proof of that. It's no exaggeration to say that after embarking on my first property investment, I've more or less been on vacation ever since. Real estate investment gives me everything I need to pay the bills, plan for the future, and cover the little extras that make life worth living. I still maintain my credentials as a financial planner, but real estate has allowed me to be very selective about the clients I now take on.

Most importantly, it gives me freedom with my time. I don't have to cut the best moments short in order to get to work. I don't have to ask my boss's permission to take a few weeks off. I don't have to choose between time enjoying my family and time providing for my family. As simplistic as it might sound, owning real estate is the quickest, most reliable method I've found to make sure I'm in charge of my money instead of money being in charge of me.

If you're ready to stop daydreaming about freedom and make it a reality, it's time to take the first step. The next chapter will show you how.

Chapter 2

Start with the End in Mind: Exit Strategies for Profit

I recently learned a surprising statistic: the average person in North America lives within about $200 of their monthly budget. In other words, every month finds them about $200 behind or ahead of what they need to pay their bills.

Sure, $200 isn't enough to completely change your way of life. But it is enough to keep you in a perpetual state of anxiety…or to let you breathe a big sigh of relief.

Just take a moment to think about what you'd do if you had an extra $200 per month.

Would you put it into long-term savings?

Would you take your spouse out for a nice meal?

Would you save it up over several months and spend it on a great vacation with your family?

Would you use it as an emergency fund, in case you had trouble paying the bills or some unexpected expense came up?

What you'd do with that extra cash is up to you. It's less about what you use it for, and more about the difference it makes to the quality of your day-to-day life. While $200 might not sound like much, it really can be the difference between worrying about whether a given expense is cutting into some other part of your budget, and being able to just relax and enjoy life.

Of course, you could probably make an extra $200 per month easily just by staying a couple hours later at the office or getting a second job on the weekends. What really makes the difference in this scenario is when you don't have to do any extra work for it. No side job. No overtime. No crossing your fingers for a bigger-than-average commission. Just living your life the same as always, but with the edge of anxiety taken off and the ability to breathe a little more freely.

As I've said before, real estate investment isn't about getting super rich, super fast. It's about freeing up your time so that you can spend less of your life working (and worrying) and more of it living.

Just Imagine

Now try stretching your imagination a little bit further. What might it be like to not have to do what you do every Monday to Friday, from 9 to 5?

What if you didn't have to meet with clients?

What if you didn't have to pick up the phone when it rang?

What if you didn't have to sit through presentations or file quarterly reports?

If it's hard for you to imagine, I get it. We've all been conditioned to believe that time equals money—in other words, the only way to get X amount of dollars is to put in Y amount of time.

But that's completely wrong. Despite what you may have been taught, life does not have to be that way.

Making Money While You're Asleep

Consider this quote from the famed British photographer David Bailey:

> "To be rich, you have to be making money while you're asleep."

It sounds like a joke, but it's actually very insightful. Most hard-working middle-class people spend their day chasing an income until they're exhausted, then catch a few hours of sleep, only to get up and do it all again the next day. The rich, on the other hand, spend their waking hours accumulating assets— channels that automatically generate cash for them—without having to do any extra work. These multiple streams of automatic money, also known as "passive income," are the key to building wealth.

It's true that a good stock portfolio will accomplish the same thing, at least for a while. But as we saw earlier, the big problem with this strategy is how the stock market fluctuates. There's no consistency to it, no way to be sure that investing X dollars today will yield Y dollars when you're ready to cash out.

In contrast, being invested in a successful business gives you not only an income stream, but also a measure of influence and control over the consistency of that income. As long as you've got the materials coming in on one end, you can be sure of the desired outcome on the other end. If something fluctuates, you can go in and fine-tune how you're doing business so that things keep clicking along the way they're supposed to.

You'll hear me say this often throughout this book, but real estate investment is essentially a business in a box. Basically, everything you need to be successful is intuitively available to you right from the time you purchase the property. Once that is done, all you really have to do is advertise and fill the property, then sit back and collect cheques.

Of course, I'm exaggerating the simplicity of it to some degree. But buying a well-researched property to rent isn't much more complicated than that. Unlike the mysterious forces behind the stock market that make a mutual fund's value go up and down, owning a rental property works on the same principles as a lemonade stand. You're meeting a basic human need, and the more value you put into it, the more value you'll get out of it.

It's Not About Getting Rich (Not at First, Anyway)

I get the sense that when people initially look into real estate investing, it's with the idea of becoming rich. If that's what you want, that's totally fine. Real estate can indeed be a vehicle for getting rich—it just won't happen overnight like winning the lottery or having one of your stocks suddenly skyrocket.

Remember, however, that both the lottery and the stock market depend completely on luck. You can't have any certainty of how or when they will pay off for you. Moreover, in the case of the stock market, you're faced with the uncertainty of whether to hold onto that skyrocketing stock and see if the value goes further up, or to sell now while the market is hot. It all comes down to guesswork.

Real estate, on the other hand, takes almost no guesswork. A rental property is not only a business in a box, but it's a business with a built-in customer base.

Ask anyone who has ever started their own company, and they'll tell you that the hardest part is finding customers. But there's always going to be somebody looking for a place to live, whether for the short term or the long term. All it usually takes to attract that customer is placing a couple of ads online, vetting the possible candidates, and choosing the one who seems most likely to take care of your investment. At that point, it's just a matter of checking in periodically to make sure your property is still standing.

Unlike a regular job, you get to decide how much time you spend on real estate investment. You can do it all day, every day, or you can come back to it once a week (or once a month, or even once every few years when a tenant moves out and a new one moves in). While it's not, strictly speaking, a passive way of creating wealth, it's very close. It's money coming into your pocket without you having to put in any extra work if you don't want to. In fact, I have clients who have never even seen the houses they've invested in!

The Built-In Savings Machine

It always surprises people when I admit that I'm a horrible saver. Yes, I'm a financial planner, which means I should know better. However, I have what I like to call "shiny toy syndrome." I wish I had the discipline to take a certain percentage of my money and put it into savings. But the reality is that if I've got access to money, it's probably going to get spent.

That's part of what makes real estate the perfect investment for me—it has a built-in savings component. When I collect rent from tenants each month, I know that I can't just go out and spend those checks. Growing my investments requires putting a percentage of my rental income back into the home for maintenance, taxes, insurance and all the rest. My investments force me to be financially prudent. It's a pretty great side benefit.

At the same time, though, investing in real estate fulfills my shiny toy compulsion in a very obvious way: by incentivizing me to look for more properties to buy. I love scouting the market for homes that need love, putting in the work to make them beautiful, and seeing people's "I want to live here" reactions when the renovations are done. The fact that I can make a lot of money doing all this is just icing on the cake.

However, you don't have to share my passion for DIY renovation (or my weakness for buying shiny new stuff) in order to make a lot of money for yourself. There are multiple ways to build wealth in real estate investment, and only one of them involves any hands-on work.

Start with Your Exit Strategy

This chapter has been all about the big-picture "why" of real estate investing, because getting what you want from real estate investment requires you to keep your end goal in mind. When you're investigating potential properties to buy, your desired outcome should dictate everything about where you start. In the next chapter, we'll talk about how those goals help you pick the approach to real estate investment that will guarantee you the success you want.

Chapter 3

The Six Real Estate Investment Profit Paths

Think back to that extra $200 per month we talked about in the last chapter. If you had that extra income, what would you like it to accomplish for you?

Maybe you'd like to build a legacy for your family by creating a stream of income that you can pass on to your kids after you're gone.

Maybe you're eager to amass wealth as quickly as possible, so you can quit that job you hate.

Maybe you've got outstanding bills that you're making the minimum payments on and you'd like to get those out of your life for good.

Maybe you just want a little extra income so that you don't have to choose between enjoying a nice dinner once a month and taking your family on an annual vacation.

Whatever your goal is, there's an approach to real estate investment tailor-made to help you fulfill it.

What Will Make It Worth Your While?

Unlike other forms of investing, real estate doesn't come in a one-size-fits-all model. The approach you choose offers a unique combination of financial outlay, personal involvement, and amount and frequency of return.

And in total, there are six ways to make money in real estate investment, which I call the Six Profit Paths:

1. Buy-and-Hold
2. Rent-to-Own
3. Fix-and-Flip
4. Sandwiched Lease Option
5. Wholesaling
6. Land Investment

When you talk about real estate investing to most people, they almost always think of #3, the Fix-and-Flip, where somebody buys a dilapidated house, makes it nice, and sells it for a major markup.

Why?

Because it's what you see in countless TV shows.

Now, it's definitely a good approach to real estate investment if your goal is to get in and out quickly (though it has to be said that in real life, it looks nothing like it does on TV). However, Fix-and-Flip is far from the only approach.

There's no right or wrong Profit Path in real estate investing. It's just a matter of matching your criteria for a successful return (in terms of money and equity) with how much you wish to be involved (or not) in managing the asset day-to-day. Do you need a big lump sum return up front, or do you want a steady cashflow over the next several years? If you want the big immediate payout, are you willing to hold onto the property indefinitely until you find a buyer?

Each Profit Path offers a different trade-off of time, effort, personal investment and financial return. Not every Profit Path listed here will make sense for you—it all depends on how you define the success of your investment. The criteria you have for how it fits into your life, and what you're willing to do as the owner of this business in a box, will dictate how you maximize your investment.

Choose the Approach That Works for You

Buy-and-Hold

Buy-and-hold can be one of the simplest Profit Paths to implement. You simply buy a turnkey property and begin renting it out.

Compared to the Fix-and-Flip that you'll read about below, you bring in smaller amounts of money each month rather than a single big cash payout. It's not hard to find a good property for a buy-and-hold—just look down the street from where you live. The only thing to consider is whether the numbers make sense. To me, this just means having a decent amount (even just $50) left in my pocket after expenses are paid.

An important note about Buy-and-Hold is that holding on to the property yourself means you're responsible to maintain it. However, even that can be modified depending on your needs, skills, and interests. As I said, I like doing the maintenance work on my own properties. But for investors who prefer to be more hands-off, there are third-party property managers they can retain who will do the maintenance for them.

I've heard people say that they object to property managers because they are "too expensive." That is a short-sighted way to look at it. Whether to hire a property manager or not is a question of money versus time: do you want to keep 100 percent of the profits from the property while spending more time on it, or would you rather keep a slightly smaller percentage of the profits while spending less time? Again, there's no "right" answer—it just depends on what best fits your needs. The key point is, whether or not you hire a manager, you'll still have more money than you did before you invested.

The other thing to know about the Buy-and-Hold Profit Path is that it's a long game. The longer you hold the property, the larger the financial return is likely to be. If you purchase a property that earns $400 to $500 per month and hold it for five years, you will also probably accumulate a significant amount of equity that you can then access by refinancing your mortgage or taking out a second mortgage. Like any other loan, that money can be pulled out tax-free. In other words, every five years or so, you can potentially reap a bonus of between $25,000 and $100,000 tax-free (obviously, depending on what's happening in the market at that time). That's a pretty fantastic return, not to mention the satisfaction of being able to tell the government, "No, no. This is all mine, thank you very much."

Who couldn't use an extra $25,000 here and there?

The true moneymaking component in real estate is time—not just having the asset but having it over a good period of time. Buy-and-Hold is as simple as its name suggests: the longer you hold a property, the more equity you'll accumulate and the more money you'll be able to extract.

Rent-to-Own

Rent-to-own—also known as "lease option"—is the Profit Path that got me started in real estate investment. In this approach, you rent your property to a tenant who eventually intends to buy the property from you at an agreed point in time. In the interim, they pay you rent and build a deposit.

Compared to simply renting the property out, Rent-to-Own tends to attract a higher quality of tenant—people who expect that the home will one day be their own will treat it with an extra level of care and respect. They might even put their own money into it in the form of added improvements or renovations, since they're hoping to create some equity in that property for themselves.

> I had a rent-to-own tenant ask me if they could finish the basement in the home they were renting from me. I told them that as long as they hired a licensed contractor for the job (i.e., not a friend with a toolbelt) and secured all the necessary permits, I had no objection.

> Having them take on improvements not only reduced my overall investment risk, but also increased my equity in the property. If for some reason the tenants walked away from our Rent-to-Own agreement, having a finished basement would only increase the monthly rent I'd be able to charge...with no additional cost or effort from me. What property owner would say no to that?

There are different variations of Rent-to-Own, but in the model that I use, a portion of the monthly rent is credited toward the down payment needed to purchase the property. Most Rent-to-Own tenants are people who don't have the ability to buy a home following the "normal" procedure. Rather than spend months or years trying to save up enough for a down payment, they can move into the house right away and pay a little extra in rent each month (maybe 20 to 30 percent more) which gets credited toward their down payment.

This is typically done through a second agreement known as an "option to buy." When you draw up the contract with the tenant, it specifies the future purchase price from tenant to landlord plus the appreciation value. There's also typically an up-front payment called an option to buy fee—it's essentially an extra-large rental deposit that functions like a mini-down payment for the property.

Because it is assumed that the property will be sold to the tenant in the future, the contract may also specify that the tenant will be responsible for a certain amount of property maintenance. If they clog the toilet, it's up to them to get it fixed; if the light bulbs burn out, they have to replace them. However, major expenses like a leaky roof or a furnace replacement are typically still the responsibility of the landlord.

> It's important to know that Rent-to-Own can be a dou-ble-edged sword, mainly for the landlord but also for the tenant. For example, I had a Rent-to-Own property that increased in value dramatically just after the tenant and I had agreed the final purchase price. There was no pro-vision in the contract saying that we would readjust if the market had an uptick.
>
> When the tenants actually did buy the house three years later, an identical house down the street sold for about $200,000 more than what they paid me. As you can im-agine, that was a horrible night for me as an investor. I still made money, but I was haunted for a while by how much I *could* have made.

The moral of the story is *Let the seller beware.* Rent-to-Own might seem like a reliable, conservative approach to real estate investment, but even the best-laid plans can change. Market upticks aren't the only thing that can send your projections sideways. Sometimes even the best tenants don't end up fol-lowing through on the purchase. Maybe your tenants are a couple whose marriage breaks down, or one of them loses a job, or they get up and walk away in the middle of the night with no explanation, leaving $10,000 or more of what they've invested behind them. Things like that do happen, and you have to know how to make the best of an unexpected situation. Make sure your contract is watertight, and that all credits and down payments are non-refundable.

The Fix-and-Flip

I won't lie—taking care of a property can be frustrating. Getting the work done is a challenge, of course, but the biggest issue is always dealing with tenants. In Chapter 7 we'll talk about strategies for finding quality tenants, but even with the best due diligence, you've got to be ready to deal with the occasional difficult tenant, and even the possibility of evictions.

The Fix-and-Flip Profit Path protects you from that eventuality. You're not dealing with tenants, nor with the issues that arise from holding a property long-term. You simply purchase the property, fix it up, find somebody to buy it, and collect the return on your investment.

There are tax consequences for doing that, which means that Fix-and-Flip isn't always best as a serial investment, and it's important to be aware that using this approach multiple times will alert the authorities that you're running a business, and they'll tax you based on 100 percent of your profit. However, if you use Fix-and-Flip on a one-off basis, only 50 percent of the money you make is taxable as a capital gain. The other 50 percent is tax-free. Other than the refinancing scenario outlined in Buy-and-Hold above, this is probably the best tax scenario you can put yourself in.

The challenge of Fix-and-Flip is that you have to find the right house. It should be a house that you can buy for below the market average, put a minimal amount of work into, and sell for maximum profit.

With Buy-and-Hold, you can just do the minimum amount of work required (if any) on the property to get the right tenant, then keep renting it until you make back your investment. But with Fix-and-Flip, if you don't buy the right property at the right price, there's no guarantee that somebody will pay the price you need to make back what you spent plus the profit that you have in mind.

Because the intention is to make your profit all at once instead of incrementally, it's critical to keep a grasp on your budget and to be very strategic in the kind of renovations that you do. Remember, you're not on HGTV. You have to think about the general taste for improvements—what are most people likely to want? If you spend a lot of money on boutique upgrades that suit a very small niche of people, you could be jeopardizing your ability to sell that property in a timely manner.

For example, spending $50,000 to add an in-ground swimming pool gives tremendous "wow factor" to a home but adds very little financial value. The same amount spent adding a garage or even an attached work shed, however, can push your house into a whole new price bracket in which people are willing to pay more.

> A swimming pool is only truly valuable as an addition to people who value a pool...and those are a lot rarer than you might think. Indeed, most buyers see a pool as a liability.

The bottom line is that Fix-and-Flip is the best approach if you need a large sum of money quickly. Personally, I've used

Fix-and-Flip to generate up to $160,000 in as little as eight months.

> One of my favorite forms of investing is a hybrid of the Buy-and-Hold and Fix-and-Flip Profit Paths referred to as the BRRR Method—Buy Renovate Refinance Rent.
>
> Like a Fix-and-Flip, you buy a dilapidated property and renovate it to increase its value, but then rather than selling it immediately at a markup, you refinance to take out as much of your initial capital as you can and then rent it out so that somebody else pays off your mortgage and creates cashflow. It's a clever, creative strategy that lets you reap the benefits of both models at once.
>
> Ideally, in the BRRR Method you are attempting to extract all the principal you invested upfront. Unfortunately, this is becoming more and more unlikely as banks demand more equity to reduce their risk. That said, I have found that the BRRR Method locks up far less of your upfront capital than buying a turnkey renovated property.

Sandwiched Lease Option

A Sandwiched Lease Option is an interesting Profit Path—although it is one that I personally have not used yet. In many respects, it works like Airbnb: Airbnb is the largest rental company in the world, and yet it owns no property.

To set up a Sandwiched Lease Option, you need two other parties: a property owner (who is an independent third party), and someone who wants to rent that property.

First, you approach the property owner and negotiate three things: a fixed rent, the ability to sublease the property to a third party, and the option for you to buy the property at some point in the future. It's attractive for them because in exchange for the option to buy while you're leasing that property, you are guaranteeing the owner an agreed income in. They know that they'll always get paid their rent, and they have someone else taking care of the property for them to some degree.

The second part of the deal is that you sublease the house to a tenant. Of course, to make this profitable for you, that has to be at a higher rent than what you're paying the owner.

Why do you need to negotiate an option to buy the property in the future? Because there are two ways to make this Profit Path work.

One way is to use the property as a furnished short-term rental (such as an Airbnb), which allows for higher rents than "normal" rental, so you can make the deal profitable immediately. Then, because the property has a track record of generating above average cashflow, it'll be worth more when you come to sell it in the future.

The other way is to find a tenant who wants to buy the property in the future, but for whatever reason can't get a traditional mortgage right now. You can offer them a Rent-to-Own deal as outlined above, which also allows you to charge the higher rent needed to make this profitable.

One of the challenges to making this work is coordinating the date when you can buy the property and the agreement you make with the new tenant on when they can buy it. In an ideal world, everything will happen in the space of a few days (rather than the typical real estate cycle of weeks or months!).

In this investment model, you're basically a middleman between the person who actually owns the property and a Rent-to-Own tenant who wants to buy the property eventually. You're making money on the difference between the rent you pay your landlord and what you're getting from your sublet tenant.

Better still, since you don't own the property, you don't have to put in a down payment. You've got positive cashflow coming in without even owning the house. Also, when it comes time to sell the property in the future, your option-to-buy agreement will typically have a built-in equity component that you'll be able to cash in when you sell to the new tenant.

As long as it's a win-win situation, the Sandwiched Lease Option is a fantastic way to get into managing real estate and potentially make a lot of money in a short period of time. For example, let's say you find a one-bedroom condominium for sale in Toronto's Arts District, where rent is easily upwards of $2,000 per month. A property like that could easily cost $480,000 to buy, which means a down payment of at least $96,000 (assuming it's an investment).

You might not have that kind of cash on hand, but if you're able to convince the owner to rent-to-own the condo to you, and you guarantee that they will get their monthly rent no matter what happens, that the property will be taken care of, and that you'll buy the property at some point within the next two years for a predetermined price, you could then turn around sublease the condo (probably in a Rent-to-Own deal of your own) to someone who will be paying as much as $3,000 per month.

On your side, you might be making $300-$800 per month and then potentially cash out another lump sum when the condo is sold within that two-year timeframe. And you didn't have to put down a dime—all you had to spend was the cost of an ad, the time to negotiate, and maybe the legal fees for the appropriate contracts to get this done.

Wholesaling

Where the Sandwiched Lease Option puts you, the investor, as the middleman between a landlord and a tenant, Wholesaling puts you between the seller and the buyer of a property.

As the principal investor, you go out and find the deal, get a sales agreement on paper, then find someone else to step in and complete the sale, and your reward is a finder's fee or an additional premium on the sale price. It's a great model to consider if you're good at finding property deals and you have a strong network of potential buyers.

I had a situation where a seller's house was under power of sale. A series of events had left him unable to pay his mortgage on time, and he got to the point where the bank was ready to force the sale of his house in order to get their money back.

The seller contacted me based on my Rent-to-Own ads. He was hoping I would buy the property and then rent back to him, so he and his family could go on living there.

Because it was under power of sale, the property was being offered at an incredible price. I had my hands full with my other rental properties at that time and I wasn't in a position to take on another, but it was too good a deal to pass up. So, I took on the contract to buy the house and then immediately began searching for someone to finish the transaction.

It didn't take me long to find an investor in my network. I assigned the contract to him and collected a $5,000 finder's fee for my role in the deal, while he took on the transaction and assumed the role of property owner. He agreed to operate under the Rent-to-Own model, so the seller and his family were not only able to keep living in the house, but also had a chance to reclaim ownership down the road. It was a win for everyone.

Land Investment

Investing in land can be by far the longest game of all the Profit Paths listed here. It requires a lot of foresight about how your city is growing, as well as a sixth sense for which will be the next area to get developed. In essence, you're betting on urban sprawl. For example, if you're buying farmland five to ten miles outside the city limits, you're trusting that within the next several years the city will expand so far that developers will need to buy that land from you (unless you plan to develop it yourself).

Land investment offers many advantages over investing in buildings. There are no tenants to deal with, no renovations to do, no maintenance costs. It's property investment without the headaches.

The downside is that it requires a fair amount of insight and/or correct guesswork—the last thing you want is to buy hundreds of open acres, only to find nobody is interested in buying them.

It's also impossible to know how long it will take for your investment to pay off.

As a financial planner, I had a client who owned 18 acres in the Greenbelt, a protected nature area that surrounds the western portion of Lake Ontario from Oshawa to Niagara Falls. He was approached by a builder who offered to buy the property at $250,000 per acre.

It was an incredible price, given that no development was allowed on the property. But the builder was anticipating that at some point in the future, the city would grow so much that the government would lift its restrictions on development in the Greenbelt.

He may or may not be right. More than 100,000 people move into the Greater Toronto Area every year—that's 1.8% per year, which is faster than the entire state of Texas is growing—and that number is expected to increase well into 2021. Legislators are already discussing the issue of finding more land to house all these incoming residents.

Will the builder's gamble pay off in the next few years? Or will the Greenbelt remain a no-development zone? It could go either way. That's the risk of land investment. But if you're willing to do your research and be patient, this model can ultimately yield significant payoffs.

Mix-and-Match

Of course, there's no rule that says you can't use multiple Profit Paths at the same time to get a good mix of short- and long-term results. Personally, I use several different Profit Paths in my real estate portfolio.

As I write this book, I have a duplex that I operate under the Buy-and-Hold model, which brings in $800 per month after all the property expenses are paid. That's a great, steady income stream, one that requires very little work on my part.

I also have a student rental property, which I rent out by the room. Each of the six rooms goes for $500 to $600, which magnifies the positive cashflow of that property three or four times. However, students aren't the most conscientious tenants in the world, so the student rental requires a lot of added work for upkeep.

> Think also about how much of a down payment you want to put in at the outset. Any house can be made to generate cashflow—the amount just depends on the size of your down payment. Most people put down the smallest amount possible, in order to maximize their rate of return on the property.
>
> But if, on the other hand, you want to maximize the month-to-month income your property brings in, putting in a greater down payment will reduce your mortgage payments and put more of the rent in your pocket each month.

Start at the End

When you approach real estate investment, it's not enough just to want to make money. That's how people get into trouble— they rush ahead with whichever model they're already familiar with and fail to consider the specific outcomes they want.

The key to success in real estate investment is to start at the end, not at the beginning. You need to get very granular about exactly what you want out of your investment.

Ask yourself what's important to you, what you want to achieve, and what kind of challenges you're willing to deal with for the return. Do you want a little extra money every month, and if so, how much? Are you looking to make yourself a big chunk of money in a small timespan? Do you want to pay off debt, save for retirement, leave a legacy for your kids?

Answering these questions gives you much-needed clarity on what investment success looks like for you and allows you to match your needs and values with the investment Profit Path that offers you the greatest reward.

Chapter 4

Misconceptions About Real Estate Investing

I have my father to thank for introducing me to real estate investment, but it was my father-in-law who taught me how to answer the doubts and objections people have about it.

My wife's parents, like mine, are immigrants who worked hard all their lives—my father-in-law in construction, my mother-in-law in the mail room of a university. Coming from a background in farming, their work ethic was as straightforward as can be: you get back what you put in. They were 9-to-5 people who kept their eyes on the pension that would be theirs after the requisite thirty years.

They were also scrupulous savers—we joked that my father-in-law's wealth management strategy consisted of shoving bundles of cash under his mattress. His idea of splurging was buying Heinz ketchup instead of a generic brand. It goes without saying that investing for the sake of a better retirement, much less improving their lifestyle, would never have occurred to him.

My father-in-law's outlook was in complete contrast to how I was brought up. My dad was a real estate agent who constantly bought and sold properties on his own. He was always talking about the latest deal he had in the works, and as the oldest child, I was his sounding board. From a young age, I was schooled in entrepreneurship, with an emphasis on personal responsibility. If I wanted something, it was up to me to come up with the cash.

I was a good student of my dad's entrepreneurial lessons and put them into practice at an early age. Like a lot of kids, my first business was a lemonade stand. But I didn't set it up in my driveway and wait for people to walk down the street. Instead, I set up my stand in a construction zone down the road from our house. My efforts were rewarded—my mom found me hustling lemonade to a gang of thirsty laborers, their dump trucks parked nearby.

Maybe it's my upbringing, or just the temperament I inherited from my dad, but working a 9-to-5 job for somebody else never appealed to me. I've done it, but it always felt like pulling teeth. Instead, I've always been drawn toward work that gives me the freedom to set my own schedule and make as much money as I want.

The same is true for how I approach investing. Even though I directed people in very traditional, "by the book" investing strategies as part of my job, I felt sure there had to be something better. And when I reconnected with John, the investor I talked about in Chapter 1, I knew real estate investment was it.

As I began to experience success with real estate investment, I immediately wanted to share its potential with other people. It never crossed my mind that it might be a topic of conversation to avoid, especially with my wife's family. As a financial planner, I talked about money all the time, and now that I was excited about the potential of this new strategy, I wanted to share it with them.

One night after a big family dinner, when my father-in-law and I were the only ones left at the table, I mentioned my plan to build up a portfolio of properties that would provide us with ongoing rental income. To my surprise, my father-in-law snapped. He began shouting at me that it was a terrible idea. He insisted that I'd end up sinking all my money in repairs and maintenance, that the tenants would destroy our properties, on and on.

I was completely thrown. I tried to explain where I was coming from, but with each attempt I made, he got angrier, to the point where he was so upset that he was shaking. I was completely taken aback—I'd never experienced that level of anger from him before (and haven't since).

Even though the closest my father-in-law had ever come to real estate investment was buying and selling his own house, he talked about it as though he'd been through it all himself—the "money pit" property, the horrible tenants, etc.

In retrospect, it's not hard to understand why all he knew (or thought he knew) about real estate investment were the potential downsides. He'd clearly heard stories like these from other property investors. And judging by the stories they'd told him, they either didn't know what they were doing, or they just enjoyed complaining. Again, that's understandable—tenant horror stories are a lot more fun to share with your friends than saying that life is great, you don't have any worries about paying your bills, and your tenants are nice people.

Ultimately, my father-in-law's attitude toward real estate investment was based on what he was comfortable with. Some people (me included) might look at his practice of stuffing money under the mattress as crazy. He, on the other hand, saw putting money into rental properties as crazy.

No investment strategy is perfect. You have to find the one that works best for you. I was going into real estate investment knowing the risks and responsibilities it brought, and ready to make the best of it. That's what has ultimately made me successful at it. I was under no illusions, but to me, the potential rewards outweighed the risks, and I was ready to accept the responsibilities.

To this day, I still don't think that my father-in-law knows what exactly my work entails. But it doesn't enrage him the way it did that day. He's seen the difference real estate investment has made in our family's life, and while he probably won't ever get into it for himself, he can't deny that we're onto something good.

Are the Problems Worth the Payoff?

People's misconceptions about investing in real estate are usually based on horror stories they've heard from somebody who didn't approach it the right way. Maybe they thought it would make them rich overnight. Maybe they bought a property that needed too much work or wasn't in a good location. Maybe they were too quick to accept a tenant without proper vetting. Maybe they were naïve about the returns they should expect or the effort they needed to put in.

Anything you do in life—whether it's work, investing, a relationship, you name it—will inevitably bring you up against problems to solve. Real estate investment, like everything else, brings its challenges. No matter how much you read about it before getting started, you're never going to eliminate all the possible problems. It's not a question of *if* you'll have to replace a broken furnace or evict a sloppy tenant, it's *when*.

Rather than trying to eliminate all possible problems, you need to focus on eliminating your misconceptions *before* you start to invest.

For example, my parents made the mistake of believing they always had to do everything themselves when it came to maintaining their properties. At the height of their investing, they had ten properties—that meant ten different people could call my parents directly if a light bulb blew out or the plumbing sprang a leak. No wonder they decided they'd had enough. Unfortunately, they chose to sell off all their properties rather than the obvious solution of hiring a property manager to take the day-to-day work off their plates.

I know what my parents' rebuttal to that idea would be: property managers are too expensive. It's true that hiring a property manager would mean parting with between five and ten percent of their gross rent. But, as I said in Chapter 3, the way to look at it is not that they're giving someone else ten percent to do something they could do themselves, but rather that they are keeping 90 percent of those profits along with their sanity.

To this day, my dad still regrets having sold all his properties. He didn't take the time to step back and reassess his approach. Instead, he and my mom let their emotions dictate the solution, which was to divest themselves of everything.

Clearing Up Common Misconceptions

I talk with a lot of people who are interested in real estate investment, and there is definitely a pattern when it comes to the misconceptions that people have.

Misconception #1: "I need a lot of money to get into real estate."

This is by far the biggest misconception I encounter. It's true that you do need to have access to large sums of capital. However, that capital doesn't have to come out of your savings. It can just as easily be borrowed money, whether it be a credit card, a line of credit, or a mortgage. As long as you have the ability to access it, you can begin the process of investing in real estate.

When I purchased my last property, I put just $5,000 of my own money into the deal. Everything else was borrowed. Yes, I have to pay for the debt I took on, but that is much easier to do in the short-term than waiting until I've put away enough for a down payment. Saving up $70,000 or more takes a long time when you're only putting away a hundred dollars from each paycheck. At that rate, you might as well just be investing according to the traditional route.

The thing is, it's much easier than most people realize to find someone else out there who is sitting on a big pile of money and wondering what to do with it. I know that sounds funny, but there are people like that out there.

For example, a few years back I was approached by an investor who had roughly $200,000 invested in a mutual fund and was looking for a less volatile investment. He liked the sound of real estate, but definitely did not want to manage a property— he wanted his money to do the hard work for him. I suggested he invest through a joint venture partnership with my firm, Magellan Wealth Management. Using his funds as capital, we purchased a property, renovated it and turned it into a multi-family home. After about five years of renting it out, my firm proposed buying him out with our portion of the equity and profits that the property had accumulated over that time. The agreement benefited everyone—we were able to add one more property to our portfolio by leveraging our expertise as opposed to our bank account, and he enjoyed a return of about 15 percent a year with no work or worry on his end.

A New Way to Think About Mortgages

Most people have been schooled in the mindset that once you've paid off your house, you don't touch it ever again. But that is an incredibly limiting way of thinking. For most people, their home is the greatest resource that they never tap. Letting your equity sit there idly while you scrimp and save for retirement is, to me, a terrible opportunity to miss.

Take the average Canadian who bought a house for $350,000 five years ago. In Canada, when you buy a principal residence, you have to put down at least 5 percent of the purchase price in cash (investment property requires a minimum down payment of 20%)—so this homeowner put down $17,500 and has a mortgage of $332,500, on which they're paying $1379.12 per month (assuming an interest rate of 2.85% and a 30 year amortization). (Please note that we ignored CMHC mortgage insurance in these calculations.)

Now assume that the market had gone up steadily by just 3 percent per year—roughly the average national rate of appreciation across Canada. That means their house is now worth $405,745.92 and their equity has grown from $17,500 to $110,822.75—that's a huge jump!

Let's say this average Canadian homeowner finds somebody like myself who needs to borrow $50,000 for a short period of time and is offering them an 8 percent interest rate. On $50,000, that would yield $4,000 in just one year.

Sounds like a good opportunity, right? But as an average Canadian, they don't have much extra cash just hanging out in their chequing account. The only real asset they have is the equity in their house. Without selling their home, though, the only way to access this equity is via a home equity line of credit or a mortgage refinance.

To keep the calculation as simple as possible, we will assume these people refinance their mortgage at the same rate they had before (2.89%) and reset the amortization period to 30 years. Assuming they refinance up to 85% loan-to-value, they will be able to extract just under $50,000 which they can now put to work.

> When you start investing in real estate, you'll hear the term "loan to value" or LTV used quite a bit in conjunction with a percentage when discussing financing. LTV represents the size of the mortgage in relation to the overall value of the property. In the example above, when we say a property valued at $405,745.92 is refinanced to 85% loan-to-value, it means the mortgage is now $344,884.03. (405,745.92 x 0.85 = 344884.03)

Now put yourself in the shoes of this average Canadian homeowner. How would you feel in that scenario, having made over $4,000 in just one year without having had to do anything but lend someone money?

> You might be thinking that lending money as an investment is a risky idea. But consider what you are actually doing when you "invest" your money into stocks or mutual funds. No matter what form of investment you choose, it all boils down to the same thing: lending money in the hope that it will make you more money.

Even with an extra $4,000 on the table, of course, some people still raise objections.

Objection #1: "That's not a huge amount of money."

True. On the other hand, it's more money than you had before. Trust me when I say you'll be surprised at how much impact that little bit extra has on your life, not to mention how fast it can snowball if you stay the course.

Objection #2: "If I increase my mortgage by $50,000, I have a bigger payment now."

True again, but not by much. The fact is that your payment would only be increased by 4 percent—with the numbers we're discussing here, that means an increase of just $51.36 per month. With your 8 percent interest rate, that still leaves a profit of $281.97 per month.

It's worth noting that the numbers in this scenario are extremely conservative. In reality, the interest rate offered on a private mortgage such as this can be greater than 8 percent and, thanks to leveraging, the rate of return is magnified tremendously. In the above example, the investor's return on investment is 549%.

Misconception #2: "Everybody knows that tenants destroy rental properties."

This isn't as certain as you assume. As we'll discuss in more detail in Chapter 7, the obvious way to avoid this is to invest in a good property in a desirable location, to have standards for the tenants you'll accept, and to vet your applicants carefully. Taking the first person who shows up without doing any due diligence is like going to a used car dealership and paying the lowest asking price you see without doing any research or even

taking a test drive. I have a very strict process that I put potential tenants through. As a result, after ten years of investing in
real estate, I still haven't had to evict anybody.

> This is a lesson that many first-time real estate investors,
> including me, have to learn the hard way.
>
> While I'm usually very careful with selecting tenants for
> my properties, there was one time during the writing of
> this book when I skirted my own rules. I had a lot on my
> plate at the time, and I was in too much of a hurry to
> carefully check all the boxes on my list.
>
> Sure enough, I ended up with a tenant who thought they
> were running the show. While they didn't destroy the
> house and always paid their bills on time, it wasn't the
> best fit and we ran into one issue after another until we
> finally parted ways. As the saying goes, when the tail
> tries to wag the dog, sometimes the dog has to bite the
> tail.

Setting up a good system for vetting tenants isn't a big mystery—it's actually quite intuitive. In many ways, it's like hiring
someone to work in your company or babysit your kids. Personally, I like to meet all my tenants and have a conversation
with them. You don't have to know them at an intimate level,
and you certainly don't have to be friends with them, but a
short conversation can usually reveal what type of person they
are.

You'd be shocked how unguarded people can be when meeting
their potential landlord. I went to meet a potential tenant at
his current home recently. As he was showing me through the

apartment, I noticed red splotches running up the wall and onto the ceiling.

I asked him, "What is that?"

He laughed, "Funny story: we were having a party and dancing around, and somebody hit a bowl of salsa that splattered all over."

I asked the obvious question, "How long ago was this?"

His answer: "Oh, about two weeks ago."

I thought, *Two weeks have gone by and you still haven't cleaned up the salsa stains?* Right away, I knew this was not the kind of person I want in my property. I'm not saying my tenants can't have parties, but leaving a mess for that length of time tells me a lot about him. If this person isn't going to clean up, what else are they not going do? What if the toilet backs up? Are they going to leave that for two weeks, too?

I had a similar situation when I was looking for tenants in my very first rent-to-own property. As we discussed in the last chapter, rent-to-own is a little more expensive for the tenant because a portion goes toward the down payment on the house. When the couple walked in, I noticed right away that the woman had a little bit of a twitch in her eye. The guy, meanwhile, was completely dishevelled—big shaggy beard, unkempt clothes, and his fingers were the dark orange color of a longtime smoker.

That first impression got progressively worse as the conversation went on. They couldn't even sit still while I explained how the rent-to-own program worked—their attention seemed to be constantly wandering. At one point, when I paused for breath, the woman said, "I'm no good with numbers. Can we have the house or not?" That was the moment when I thanked them for coming, saw them to the door, and crossed their names off my list. (Not before the man had a final cigarette, which he tossed onto my porch once he was done.)

This isn't about judging people. It's simply about finding a good match with someone you can rely on. If tenants aren't taking good care of themselves, it's unlikely that they will take good care of your house.

Misconception #3: "I don't have the money/skills/ expertise to fix up a house."

As I said earlier, nearly all the property flipping you see on TV is fake, manufactured for "wow" factor. This isn't just me being cynical. A friend of mine was selected to appear on one of those shows where the hosts accompany the guest in shopping for an older "fixer upper" type of home.

As it turned out, things work a little differently behind the scenes. What actually happened was that the producer told my friend, "Look, when you find the house you want, let us know, and then we'll pick a couple of other houses to film as if they were possibilities." Once my friend had chosen the property he wanted to buy, the production crew went in and made the house look worse than it was when they bought it, so that the transformation would be more dramatic.

It's true that many people make a very good living buying properties, fixing them up, and selling them. But what you're seeing on TV is nothing like reality. Nobody who is looking to make a profit goes into a dilapidated house and turns it into a fully modernized, gorgeously staged home. The way you make this investment work is by finding a house that needs minimal work and improving it with simple, budget-friendly options. You're going for functionality with a little finesse mixed in.

For example, I once worked with a joint venture partner who was dead set on installing a massive chandelier that would cost about $10,000 in the entryway of a house we were flipping. His argument was that it would give the house a lot of "wow factor."

True, it was a very beautiful chandelier that would make your jaw drop, but it didn't add any tangible value that would improve our bottom line. I suggested that we take about half that money and add a bedroom to the house. Adding the bedroom would push our property into the purview of a totally different potential buyer, one who had a higher budget and was looking at larger homes.

Furthermore, there's no rule that says the property owner has to be the one to break open a wall or rip out a floor. Even though I'm that rare real estate investor who enjoys doing a lot of renovation work myself, I never get involved in renovations that require a skilled expert—electrical wiring, plumbing, etc. Those are the more common issues that come with an older or fixer-upper home, and the last thing I'd recommend is trying to tackle them yourself.

The same principle applies to any aspect of property improvement that is outside your expertise or interest. If you don't have a sixth sense for picking out kitchen tiles or choosing a style of flooring, consult or hire someone who is good at it.

Misconception #4: "I don't want a second full-time job as a landlord."

Whether you're investing in real estate while working your regular job or enjoying your retirement, the last thing you want is to be constantly running over to fix leaky faucets or troubleshoot a conflict with the neighbors.

At the same time, any endeavor worth taking on involves some level of effort. To quote a friend of mine, the guy who is willing to shovel a little more shit is the one who will make more money.

That said, when I observe people in the different investment clubs that I work in, they seem to have far more stressful jobs than I do. Even major executives who make millions of dollars have to be on-site doing their job—they don't have the same flexibility that I do. Because I have that flexibility, I'm able to quickly and efficiently deal with any problems, usually by delegating them to a specialty contractor. That leaves me free to focus on the bigger fish I have to fry.

Furthermore, real estate investment involves a lot less work than most people assume. At least, it *can* be less work if you set up a good system. Success in real estate comes down to taking a realistic look at the situation, anticipating the issues that could come up, and putting systems in place to take care of those issues. In other words, it's all about mindset, preparation and planning.

I've gone ten years with just one bad tenant call—a situation where the tenants wanted to pay their rent in gift cards one month. At the time, it was a pain in the neck. Now it's just a funny story.

More common are calls about serious problems such as sewer backups, furnaces going out, and leaky roofs. These are not issues that you can put off—they have to be dealt with right away. Procrastinating usually makes the problem much worse, causing serious damage to your property, not to mention compromising the quality environment that your tenants deserve to live in.

I've received these calls at the worst possible moments (is there ever really a good time to get them?). The most egregious example has to be the time I was about to leave on vacation with my family. I was sitting on a plane, waiting for the flight attendant to tell us all to turn off our electronic devices, when a call came in about a sewer backup on one of my properties.

My first thought was an expletive I won't repeat here. But two seconds later, I sent a text to the plumber I always work with, telling him the issue and asking him to contact the tenants right away. I contacted the tenants as well, to let them know they'd be hearing from my plumber and that they should do whatever he told them. The whole thing took about five minutes, and boom—problem solved. When the flight landed, I checked back in and found out that the repair was under way.

Now, you can look at that and see it from a "glass half empty" perspective. I had to take the call when I was about to leave on vacation, and I had to spend an extra $200 or so on an emergency plumbing job. But for me, the time and the money were a drop in the bucket compared to the benefit I get from owning and renting that property. The call only took five minutes, and the expense is just part of the regular maintenance I factor into my investment.

After investing in real estate for as long as I have, I have a small army of contractors whom I trust to do all my repair jobs. That makes the distance from problem to solution especially short. But if you don't have that network established yet, it really only takes a few minutes more to Google a few options, get a few quotes, and choose the person for the job.

Perhaps you don't want to take those calls at all. That is certainly the case for a number of my investors who are retired and don't want to be bothered, which I can completely understand. To put even more distance between yourself and whatever issues come up, there's a simple solution: hire a property manager or work with a joint venture partner who can take care of all of it for you. Again, yes, there's an expense involved. But the good news is that it's a constant expense that you can factor into your investment.

As they say in the gym, "No pain, no gain." Any good result takes work. In traditional investing, that work is putting aside money each month, trusting in your broker's stock picks, and hoping it all works out to yield a number that will support your lifestyle. In real estate investment, it's spending a few minutes to make phone calls.

For many people, however, real estate investment is an unknown quantity. As a result, they tend to blow up the potential problems in their minds.

So, as you're considering whether to take the plunge into real estate investment, remember to keep the outcome in mind. Ask yourself this: if you knew ahead of time that you would get an extra $10,000 per year, how willing would you be to take on those problems? If you think about the problems in isolation, of course they sound very negative. But if you think about them in the context of what you stand to gain, meeting with a few tenants and making a few calls to repairmen might seem like a pretty good trade.

As I said earlier, it's not just about the money. Money is great, but what's really important is what that money lets you do. On the other side of a few "problem calls" is more time with your family, less anxiety about paying the bills, more opportunities to travel, and a retirement that lets you relax and enjoy life.

It's worth noting that the problems you encounter always feel trickier when you first get started. That first call from a tenant saying that their sewer backed up can really throw you off, just like it would if it was your own home's sewer that backed up. You're not expecting to have to deal with it, you didn't plan to spend money on it, you're wondering who the best person is to call, etc. But it only takes one or two situations to help you remain calm and positive and handle the situation like a pro. (And the side benefit is that it makes you better at handling these "emergencies" in your own home.)

The same goes for vetting tenants. The first time might put your stomach in knots—*Can I trust these people? Will I ever find a good renter?*—but after two or three interviews, you get a system in place and just run people through it until you find someone who checks all the boxes. In short, it only gets easier *and* the more money you make.

Creativity Is Key

If there's one thing that the past twenty or so years in Silicon Valley growth have taught us, it's that creativity is the key to successful entrepreneurship. Though it's not obvious to everyone at first, buying and selling real estate is very much the same as being an entrepreneur. Each property is a business in a box. The more creative you are, the more able you are to turn challenges into opportunities. If you're willing to be unconventional, there's no problem out there without a solution. As long as you keep a flexible mindset, the courage to tackle new challenges, and a healthy dose of creativity in solving them, you're on your way to making a lot of money.

Chapter 5

Cashflow is King

A few years back, the newspapers in my hometown of Hamilton, Ontario, were plastered with the smiling face of a local woman who'd won $10,000,000 dollars in the lottery. In the days that followed, word spread about how she was living the high life now. She bought a house in one of Hamilton's poshest neighborhoods. She got herself a nice teal Escalade and had it completely done up, complete with a huge sound system in the back. She and her husband were seen at parties all over town, blowing money like it was going out of style.

After a while, the stories died down. Then, three years later, they started up again. The former lottery winner was now dead broke, living in one of Hamilton's poorest neighborhoods, worse off than she'd been before winning her millions.

I read that story and immediately saw to the heart of the issue. The problem wasn't that the "wrong" person won the lottery. Far from it. The problem was that nobody had ever shown this woman how to manage cash.

The Benefits of Cashflow

Think back to the statistic I shared in Chapter 2 that most middle-class families are about $200 a month away from either going into debt or being able to pay their bills. That was certainly true for my own family. When my wife and I first got married, I was dipping into my line of credit every so often to make sure we covered our bills for the month. We never got into serious trouble, but it wasn't the greatest way to live. The nagging anxiety that showed up around the end of every month really ate away at me.

Buying our first rental property at that time was a big risk for us, especially as I had to refinance our home to get the down payment for the new property. But even I was shocked by how much the investment paid off. As I said before, the payoff wasn't so much in money—the rental only brought in an extra $300 a month—but in the freedom it gave us from anxiety. Just that small amount of money took so much pressure off our lives.

People like to fantasize about what they'd do if they won the lottery, suddenly having thousands upon thousands of dollars at their disposal. But the truth is that the difference they're dreaming of can be achieved by just a small increase in cashflow. Crazy, isn't it, to think that just a few hundred extra dollars each month could change your life as meaningfully as winning the lottery? And yet, it's true.

The first benefit of this small cashflow increase is stability. You're not sweating the bills anymore; you're not existing in survival mode from one month to the next; you feel like you can breathe more easily. And with that ability to breathe more easily comes a new ability to plan.

After a year of renting out that property, we were able to expand on it. Getting out of survival mode allowed us to plan a strategy for investing in a second property, which increased our cashflow even more, making an even greater difference in our lives.

Imagine you're a farmer and you've got a crop to grow. Which would be better for the crop—to get one giant rainstorm that dumps all the water you'll need for the year onto the crop in one day, or to get consistent light rain throughout the year? The answer is obvious (especially if you've ever killed a houseplant with too much water). If you flood a field with water, you might see a couple of things begin to grow for a short time. But once that water dries, everything that began to grow is going to die.

In contrast, a little rain dropping onto that field on a regular basis makes everything begin to bloom, and keeps it growing at a consistent rate. By the end of the year, you end up with a bumper crop.

That sustainable model sets real estate investment apart from any other wealth-building strategy out there.

Growth is the Goal

When they're evaluating a company, shareholders don't just look at how much revenue came in over the course of a year.

They look at how consistently that revenue appears. Why? Because life is constantly changing. There will be shifts in the systems that influence our finances that we have no control over. New policies will get passed; taxes will be reorganized; markets will rise and fall.

There's nothing you can do to fight those changes, and in most cases, there's little you can do to prepare for them. But having a small, consistent stream of revenue gives you a buffer that protects you from being heavily impacted by those changes.

The same is true for real estate investment. Having that small, consistent revenue stream provides a built-in buffer to protect your investment. Owning property necessarily involves the occasional large expense—usually at a moment when you weren't expecting it. As I said earlier, it's not a matter of *if* you're going to need a new furnace, but *when* you're going to need it. Still, it usually manages to catch people off-guard.

Having a big sum of money come in all at once can create a false sense of finality—you made the sale, and now the profits are yours. But even the biggest sums of money can go a lot quicker than you anticipate, especially if you throw in an unexpected repair or two.

Having a few hundred dollars' worth of cash flowing in each month might not sound like a huge amount of money, but when those maintenance issues arise and you have to put the furnace on a credit card, that cashflow takes a lot of the anxiety and frustration out of the situation. You don't have to sell the property because of a faulty furnace—you can address the issue without your whole financial system being jeopardized.

But perhaps the most important buffer a consistent revenue stream provides is moderating the ups and downs of your personal discipline with money. Real estate investment helps you strike a balance between risk mitigation and having the lifestyle that you want.

Rather than buying low, selling high, and suddenly getting a pile of money all at once (which can easily lead to that "lottery win" effect), a regular cashflow enables you to regularly supplement your income in a meaningful way. While it won't allow you to go out and buy a souped-up Escalade, it does help you have the lifestyle that you want. The key is consistency—having that small but regular amount each month gives you the ability to expand on the base that you started with.

Get Out of "Defensive Mode"

Somebody with zero net cashflow—not someone who is in debt, but the average person who just breaks even every month—is always in a defensive position when it comes to money. When you're constantly fighting to keep what you have, you're prevented from looking for ways to expand. But just a small increase in cashflow lets you reach from where you are to the next level. That extra few hundred dollars might be just enough to qualify you for the next opportunity.

I'm not going to argue that getting big, unexpected sums of money isn't great. Of course it is. But the person that's really going to win at the end of the day is the person who can build consistently. It's nice to have a big lake to paddle a boat around in, but you're not really going anywhere. In contrast, a steadily flowing river, no matter how slow, is going to move you forward.

You learn the hard way that a big payout feels amazing for a short time, but if that cashflow isn't sustained, that payout dries up fast, and so does the amazing feeling it brings. There have been times when I've been paid huge sums of money all at once, sometimes making more in one sale than some people will see in five years.

I won't lie—having that steep rise in my bank balance felt wonderful at the time. It was so much money that I couldn't imagine ever feeling that month-to-month anxiety again. But eventually, I looked and found that big sum of money wasn't so big anymore. As quickly as it had come, that great feeling of freedom was gone.

The time that really drove it home was after the sale of a house that brought in almost $200,000 dollars. It seemed like an incredible amount of money, but within six months, it was gone. I remember thinking, "How the hell did we spend $200,000 dollars in six months?" I hadn't bought anything crazy. I'd taken my family on just one modest vacation. The lion's share of the money had gone to taxes, bills, repairs on the rental property, this and that. By the time the last little bit of that income had been spent, I was firmly resolved never to let a big payout dazzle me like that ever again. It didn't matter how much income I gained at once time—if I didn't put it to work for me to create more cashflow, I'd be back to where I started.

The Best Defense Is a Good Offense

Most people equate discipline with pain. If it's the difference between being able to buy that shiny new toy that you want or saving 10 percent of your cashflow, most people won't go the saving route, even though we all know that we should. That little bit of cashflow gives you a stable base to grow from. It shouldn't be seen as just anything to just continuously feed your bank account with no growth to reach for

Tim Ferris has a great analogy in his book *The Four-Hour Workweek* that illustrates the power of cashflow. Let's say you wanted to buy a Ferrari. If you're like most of the people I work with, you don't have $300,000 to go and drop on a car all at once. But if you have the cashflow to make the regular payment on a car loan—which, at the average rate of 2.5 percent or 3 percent over 5 years, comes out to about $5400—your dream is in reach.

If your dream is impractical like this, more power to you. I like shiny new toys as much as the next person. But I'm guessing yours is a lot more grounded. You want to pay off debt, have some space to breathe, build a legacy for your children, or save for retirement. Think what that $5,400 per month could do for your goals.

You might be thinking $5,400 per month is still a big number. To put this in perspective, the average duplex (two apartments in one house) in my portfolio cashflows about $1,000 per month. If I want to a monthly profit of $5,000, all I have to do is find five duplexes. That's the power of cashflow over lump sums.

For me personally, cashflow has made all the difference between living on the defensive against debt and being able to pursue opportunities; between furiously treading water to keep from drowning and moving forward.

That initial $300 a month ensured that all the bills would get paid and soon allowed me to qualify for the next mortgage that added another $800 per month in cashflow to my family's life. That was a big leap—one that enabled me to buy another financial planner's practice and improved our finances to the tune of $24,000 more per year.

What started as just $300 extra per month really became an exponential blessing for my family. It was a snowball effect; one that could never have happened if I'd stayed in the defensive position, always playing catch-up.

If you came to this book with the idea of investing in a below-average property and walking out with a huge payoff, it's probably a rude awakening to hear me talking about $300 per month. This is another area in which the media representation of property investment can give people the wrong idea.

I'll be crunching the numbers for a potential client who is interested in real estate, and when they see a monthly profit of $300 or so, their face will fall.

"Oh," they'll say, "I thought I could make a *lot* of money off this."

The fact is, you can.

It just depends on how you look at it.

The Slow, Steady River Cuts the Grand Canyon

Trying to emulate an HGTV show fix-and-flip is, more often than not, a recipe for disappointment. The over-the-top expense involved in this approach creates an unhealthy urgency to find tenants or buyers in order to start recouping some of your investment.

By the same token, spending the bare minimum to fix up a broken-down property in an undesirable location usually leaves you with a property that sits empty for months. The best it can yield is a string of unreliable tenants who leave your rental worse than they found it.

The same principle is at work in both cases. When you're driven by a big lump sum payout, your choices often result in less money than you hoped for.

As enticing as it sounds to make several hundred thousand dollars all at once, it really doesn't have the same long-term impact as slow, steady cashflow. If your goal is to make meaningful changes to your lifestyle and build a sustainable financial future, you're far better off taking the "slow and steady" approach. As the saying goes, the slow and steady river cuts the Grand Canyon.

If you're willing to put in the thought and effort to build a sound structure for your real estate investments, you'll be able to kick back and enjoy consistent returns for years to come.

FREE READER RESOURCES

Knowing how much free cashflow a property is capable of generating is one of the most critical calculations in real estate investing.

To make it easier, I've created a simple calculator you can use to determine whether a deal has profit potential.

You can download it free at

www.PropertyProfitsToolbox.com

Chapter 6

Protecting Your Investment

When I'm walking a potential investor through the process of buying a rental property, I can practically set my watch for the moment when they're going to ask The Question, the one that everybody asks. As soon as the investor hears everything I have to say about the unique advantages of real estate investment, they jump in as if they've been waiting the whole time for their chance:

"But what if this housing bubble bursts?"

Agile Adaptation

The issue of market fluctuation is perhaps the most frequently asked question I get from would-be property investors. It's understandable—people are afraid of risk. The only thing they want more than *making* lots of money is to avoid *losing* money.

I tell them that real estate is the ultimate game of adaptation. It's never the same from one day to the next. As we talked about in the last chapter, government policies change, taxes go up and down, things need repair or replacing, tenants lose their jobs or get married, etc. The question isn't *whether* there will be a problem; it's *when* and *how* the problem will arise. For that reason, real estate investment requires a good deal of mental and creative agility. You must be able to adapt to a constantly changing environment.

That said, it's important not to confuse constant change with complexity. As I've been saying, real estate investing is incredibly simple to understand and navigate. Even when the economy shifts and the housing market slows down, you're going to be financially successful as long as you have that steady cashflow. If anything, a sluggish economy can sometimes provide opportunity for growth.

This is particularly true when you have a well-diversified portfolio of rentals. If one portion of your portfolio is lagging, another portion can pick up the slack. Sustainable success comes down to having no single point of failure in your portfolio.

Adapting Your Portfolio to a Shifting Market

One type of rental that often does well during a market slump is the student rental. This is because during a recession in the North American market, when people lose their jobs, they tend to go back to school. With increased college enrollment comes an increase in demand for student rentals. If you have a couple of those in your portfolio, the housing market crisis is your time to gain.

> I don't advise having only student rentals in your portfo-
> lio. While these types of rentals do tend to be very good
> for cashflow, they can also be equity traps. Banks don't
> always like to finance student rentals, since they assume
> that college-age kids (or anyone who is planning to
> move out in four years or less) is not likely to take care
> of the property.

Other rental models, such as rent-to-own, do less well during a recession. But even if that's the only model in your portfolio, that doesn't mean you're left high and dry until the economy improves. This is where creative adaptation comes into play.

For example, if your rent-to-own tenant comes to the point where they cannot afford the payments, there's nothing saying that you can't decrease their rent temporarily to keep them in the building. In my opinion, you're better off keeping good tenants who take good care of your property and are making every effort to honor your agreement than booting them out and looking for someone new. In that situation, protecting your investment means meeting them halfway. Once the financial storm passes, you can bring the rent back up to what it was. Again, the key here is keeping your eye on the long game and being able to adapt while maintaining cashflow.

The Elephant in the Room

These days, the elephant in the real estate investment room is always the 2008 housing crisis in the United States. At that time, people all over the country who had taken out enormous mortgages thanks to a credit bubble were going what they call "underwater" on those mortgages, where the house was worth less than their mortgage on it. In the worst markets, people were losing 60 percent and more of their home's value.

The one exception to this crisis was real estate investors. If you had a property that was generating positive cashflow before the market bottomed out, there was a strong likelihood that it would still keep working for you even if the mortgage was underwater. Even though the value of the asset itself might be less than the debt you had on it, it was still making money as a rental. If anything, the pool of renters was getting bigger because so many people were losing the homes they used to own.

The market value of the house was almost inconsequential—what mattered was that the cashflow was still there in some form. As a result, rental property owners were spared the full impact of the housing crisis. While others had to downsize like crazy, property investors were able to keep living the same lifestyle as they always had.

I remember speaking to a friend of mine who sold off most of his business in California and simply bought a multi-unit rental property to make up the income. By staying flexible and adjusting his plan to fit the new circumstances, he was able to weather the storm.

No Single Point of Failure

When I get started on renovating a property, I don't approach only one contractor for the job. Instead, I've built relationships with several different contractors whom I'll call on for different projects at different sites. Depending on what need to be done, I usually have a preferred person, but if they can't come when I call, I need to know I have someone else who can handle the job.

The same principle holds true for the properties themselves. The key to success is having a Plan B (and even a Plan C) for your properties and being able to easily pivot if your situation changes. Again, you want there to be no single point of failure that can bring the whole portfolio down.

For example, fix-and-flip is a great approach when the market is on the rise. But if the market takes a sudden dive, that model presents a potential problem (because time is rarely on your side in the flipping world.)

With one of my properties, I bought it intending to flip it, make a big chunk of money, and pay off a number of debts. However, I went into it with a flexible mindset. If for some reason I couldn't flip the house when I was ready, I had other options. One option was to turn it into a student rental—a natural choice since it was located only two blocks from a local college. The neighborhood also happens to be one of the most sought-after for new families in the greater Toronto area, which would also make rent-to-own a strong second option.

As it turned out, I did have to choose a different option, because by the time I had finished my work on the house, the market wasn't as friendly to the flip I'd planned on. Ultimately, though, I didn't choose any of the other options I'd considered.

Instead, my own family moved into it—as it turned out, we had a second baby on the way and needed more room.

But that didn't mean the end of my investment in the property. We ended up refinancing that house and pulling out all of the money I had put into it and then some. We bought it for $315,000, I put $50,000 worth of work into it, and once we were done, it was appraised for $435,000. Today, just three years later, a house down the street from us sold for $710,000. There's been a massive appreciation in that time, which is great news for my net worth.

So, that investment didn't go the way I'd originally planned. It worked out even better!

The key is to never go into real estate investment with just one outcome in mind. You have to have an open mind and be able to move with the market.

I grew up seeing my parents very well off in the late 1980s, only to see the massive recession of the early '90s almost wipe them out financially. It took decades for them to recover a comfortable lifestyle. And it was all because they were either unable or unwilling to adapt to the changes happening around them. For that reason, I never see failure as an option.

Diversification + Flexibility = Success

I understand that not everyone can afford to diversify their portfolio right away. For clients who are working with just one property, I advise them on how to get creative with that asset.

The key to staying strong in a shifting economy is finding ways to increase the cashflow from your property by whatever means possible.

For example, if your property has a garage, you could consider renting that space out as a storage locker. There's always someone looking for a secure place to store extra furniture or possessions, stockpile inventory for their business, park their extra car or boat, etc. Offering your property's unused space is a win/win situation—they get to store their belongings in possibly a less expensive environment than a self-storage unit, and you get a boost in your property's cashflow.

Risk mitigation gets even easier when you invest as a joint venture partner. This is the form of investment that my company, Magellan Wealth Management, specializes in. After assessing the investor's needs and financial abilities to see what kind of approach will be the best fit for them, we locate a property, negotiate the price, navigate the process of inspection and other conditions of sale, and execute a co-ownership agreement with the investor. They put up the capital and qualify for any financing needed. Legal responsibility is shared via our co-ownership agreement; we coordinate the mortgage, line up contractors and obtain permits for any updates needed, and assume all responsibility for management. Once the first set of tenants move in, any further expenses are shared 50/50.

In short, we keep as much of the actual work on our end as possible. As a result, the clients we work with have half the risk taken off their shoulders right from the beginning. If the roof blows off the house or if there's a furnace that needs to be replaced, Magellan Wealth Management fronts half of the cash required. We try to make the process as seamless for our investors as possible, to the point where they only have to show up for two things: to put up the capital for actually buying the property, and to provide the cash for any initial renovations that need to happen.

My clients aren't looking for tenants, managing tenants, or dealing with any of the issues that arise. They get all the benefits of owning the property, including the tax benefits that let them write off certain things as a business expenses, along with the four streams of income I listed in the Introduction (equity appreciation, market appreciation, mortgage pay down, and cashflow). And because we only buy houses that generate cashflow before and after renovations, and we can nimbly pivot from one model to another depending on the changes life throws at us, the only responsibility the client has is cashing their return check each month.

In fact, we've created such a seamless system that a few of our investors are fine never seeing the properties they're investing in, or only after years of steady returns. Recently, I met up with a new joint venture partner at a house we purchased in St. Catharine's, Ontario, a nearby city that is rapidly on its way up. He drove down from Toronto, toured the property, and met my contractor and designer. During our meeting, I set up a joint bank account for him, so that he can access our expense data to show his bookkeeper. My firm's objective is to be both fully transparent, so that investors can be as involved as they want to be, and fully responsible, so that our investors' only essential role is getting up off the couch to sign a legal document.

The game plan for this property was to turn it into a two-unit building to maximize the cashflow it would generate. The house we bought was a three-bedroom, two-bathroom bungalow. The inside was dated and needed a refresh.

Upstairs we simply painted the three bedrooms, swopped out the light fixtures and electrical hardware, and updated the door handles. The kitchen and bathroom got a facelift with new tiles and cabinets.

Downstairs is where most of the action happened—we gutted everything back to the concrete block foundation and started afresh. We reframed the basement, separated the electrical systems between the two apartments so each would have its own hydrometer. We also insulated it with spray-foam, not only to get the best possible comfort level for a basement apartment, but also to save a lot of time and labour cost. Our budget for all this was $90,000.

Unfortunately, we were plagued by delays and unforeseen municipal problems that ballooned our budget to $130,000 and doubled our timeline. While the delay in completion helped us achieve a higher fair market value than we had first targeted, it also meant that our investor had to leave a bit more principal than anticipated once the refinance was complete.

The upside was that this would increase the overall cashflow generated by the property, and at the rate the market was increasing, our investor would only have to wait a short period of time before we could refinance the house again to extract his remaining principal and then some.

Slow and Steady Means Success

Ultimately, risk mitigation is a combination of several factors: cashflow, property diversification, diversification of rental models, multiple exit strategies, and proper setup of your legacy. The fact that real estate investment is a long game, not a get-rich-quick scheme, is what makes it so resilient in the face of market fluctuation. By starting with a solid, steady cashflow, and working toward building a portfolio with no single point of failure, where every piece is supported by another piece, you can be confident that your investment is secure, no matter what the future brings.

Chapter 7

Recognizing Upcoming Opportunities

My wife and I took our first international vacation together before we were even married. In fact, we'd only been dating a few months. I knew that I liked her a lot, and hoped there was long-term potential in the relationship, but it definitely threw me for a loop when she emailed me at work one day to ask, "Do you want to go to Hawaii?"

My first thought was, "This girl is nuts!" Both of us were early in our careers, me in financial services and her at a travel agency. I was barely making ends meet and driving a 1991 Passat which I not-so-lovingly referred to as a massage chair on wheels. What was she thinking, proposing a "date" that would easily cost each of us $5,000?

Thinking she couldn't be serious, I emailed back a snarky reply: "Sure! If you're footing the bill, I'm in."

She told me to meet her for a coffee in five minutes. Conveniently, we worked in the same building—her office was one floor above mine, so I made it to the ground floor coffee shop first. A minute later, she stepped off the elevator and briskly walked toward me. "Okay!" she said. "We're all booked and confirmed. Our flight is a week from Thursday."

My jaw dropped to the floor. My mind began racing. *How am I going to pay for this? This girl is seriously crazy. What am I going to do now?* Some of this must have registered on my face, because she smiled and said, "Calm down and listen."

As it turned out, while researching flights for a client that morning, she'd stumbled upon some airfares that had been entered incorrectly. Somebody at the airline must have been sleeping on the job that day, because it was offering flights to Oahu at $98 plus taxes per person.

She said, "I wasn't going to wait for them to change it, so I just booked them."

By this time, my panic had transformed into excitement. I no longer thought she was crazy; I thought she was ingenious. Just by being in the right place at the right time, and seizing the opportunity when it presented itself, she'd scored us a dream vacation at an unheard-of price. She even got us steep discounts on plush hotel rooms during our visit. That's the benefit of dating a travel agent.

I've been all around the world and, to me, Hawaii is the most beautiful place on earth. The island simply takes your breath away. Even though I wasn't in real estate at the time, the island's lush beauty and trade-wind-kissed climate immediately put my property investment mentality on high alert. Lying on the pristine beaches, staring out at the incredible green scenery against the blue sky, I thought, "I need to buy a place here. I don't care if it's a shack—this is where I want to spend winters when I retire."

So, on one of our days in town, we dropped into a realty office to see what property prices were like. I probably don't need to tell you what we learned. The smallest bungalow they had listed—built decades ago, no backyard, with just two and a half feet between it and the neighboring homes—had an asking price of half a million US dollars.

To say my dreams were temporarily dashed is stating the obvious. But my sticker shock didn't last long. After all, Hawaii is an island. Their supply of developable land is limited, which already puts it at a premium. And naturally, a ton of people want this real estate. Limited supply, high demand, price goes through the roof. It's Economics 101.

This is the same reason I originally assumed that our Hawaii vacation would cost $5,000 or so. Everybody wants to fly to Oahu, but there are limited seats on the plane. If you can't afford the asking price, you have to do what my wife did: wait for an exceptional opportunity, notice something that everyone else has overlooked, and when you find it, strike immediately.

The Golden Horseshoe

The Golden Horseshoe is an area of land surrounding the western end of Lake Ontario. It is one of the most desirable areas in all of Canada. So desirable, in fact, that it's running out of land to develop. Unlike other desirable areas that can just sprawl out into surrounding neighborhoods, the Golden Horseshoe is effectively an island.

Back in 2005, the Ontario government established the Greenbelt, a natural environment permanently protected from the urban sprawl that was happening in all the cities around the lake shore. The Greenbelt surrounds Toronto from Oshawa all the way down to Niagara Falls, effectively landlocking the Golden Horseshoe.

By 2015 or so, all the areas that were still open for development within the Golden Horseshoe had been gobbled up. But at that same time, the Canadian government was opening the gates for increased immigration. That year, we had over 250,000 immigrants coming to Canada. A majority of those people came to Ontario and ended up in the Golden Horseshoe.

As you can imagine, the area is getting a little crowded. Condos and office towers have been sprouting up like wildflowers—projections of what the Toronto skyline will look like in the near future resemble Hong Kong. With limits on urban sprawl and continuously increasing demand for this area, expansion has nowhere to go but up. And so does the price of real estate.

A condo in the Toronto area went for $250,000 back in 2007. Now it goes for half a million dollars or more. This trend has spread throughout the Golden Horseshoe as more and more people are priced out of Toronto. And with the government's recently announced plans to increase immigration to 350,000 by 2020, prices will only keep increasing. Needless to say, people who saw the opportunity and bought property in the Golden Horseshoe back in 2007 are feeling pretty great right now.

FREE READER RESOURCES

Want to know about upcoming investment opportunities ahead of your competitors? Want to hear about properties that don't even get onto the MLS? As a reader of this book, you can join my Property Profits Newsletter and receive regular notifications from me about the hottest investment opportunities in the GTA.

Join at www.PropertyProfitsToolbox.com

"I Should Have Bought Here Years Ago"

Think about your favorite places in the world to visit—from cool, up-and-coming cities with a great arts district and lots of locally owned businesses, to sleepy little beach towns in Central America or Europe where the weekenders blend in with the locals. Chances are you've heard people who visit these places moaning, "Can you believe the prices of real estate? I should have bought five years ago" (or two years ago, or six months ago, or whatever the timeframe might be).

I don't have much patience for these complaints. If you don't want to be in that situation, there's an easy solution: buy right now. Stop thinking about it and dive in.

It's easy to think that property investors like me have some sixth sense for the next hot neighborhood, that we keep our ear to the ground and decode local and national news for hints as to where the next explosive investment will be. But that's just not the case. You don't have to be an expert or a psychic to know when good investment opportunities are coming.

You also don't have to wait until you find an incredible, one-in-a-million deal, or try to collect "insider tips" (if there were such a thing) that help you beat the land rush in the next hip neighborhood. As I've said, it's about being strategic—finding a modest house in a nice, clean, low-crime area, the kind of place you'd like to live in.

Do people buy practically condemned houses in blighted neighborhoods and end up selling them for incredible markups when the area becomes the next "arts district?" Yes, just like some people do fantastic renovations that send a modest house's value into the stratosphere.

Those things happen, but they are rare, and they depend more on luck than skill or strategy. You could wait all your life for a home run, but it's scoring one base hit after another that makes you a winner.

To be perfectly clear, when I say a "base hit," I don't mean a cheap property that only the most desperate tenant would want. That's a good way to end up as one of those cautionary tales you've heard. Rather, a base hit is a single-family home in an area of a city that is already well liked by the average person. A place near good schools, recreation areas, and decent shopping and where people take care of their yards. Add in a few modest improvements to make sure it's functional and aesthetically appealing, and that's all you really need to make a ton of money.

> In Canada as well as the United States, the news is constantly bewailing the shortage of "affordable housing." It's a phrase many people associate with poverty and a less desirable type of tenant. However, given the state of the North American economy, it's time to break that link.
>
> The people looking for affordable housing today are young, college-educated professionals who are on their way up, but also struggling to pay back student loans and perhaps just starting their families. By investing with this clientele in mind and setting your rentals at a price point that accommodates their needs, you're practically guaranteed a series of base hits that will make you more money faster than any upscale fix-and-flip.

As demand grows, it drives the value of even modest homes up to incredible levels. Here in Toronto, our vacancy rates are lower than anyone has ever seen. As a result, even the most unambitious property investor is making money hand over fist. One of my employees is renting out a furnished condo at a rate that would have got you a 4,000-square foot house back when I was buying my first home. It's the same all over Canada. I just learned about a proposed apartment building in British Columbia where a one-bedroom flat would go for $1,400 a month.

As the old-timers say, land is the only resource they're not making any more of. That makes it imperative to use whatever property you have efficiently, but also to get in before the competition gets fierce. (Well, fiercer than it is already.)

Going After the Base Hits

There are two stereotypical approaches to property investment: buy an old dump and fill it with people, or purchase a property and make it fancy. As we've said, the middle ground is the one we're looking for—the modest single-family home at a price point that the average professional can afford.

How do you find properties like these? The same way you probably found the home you live in now: by putting boots on the ground. The people who make great income from their property investments don't just wake up and know where to find them. They drive around the popular neighborhoods. They look at how the yards are taken care of. They talk to people they meet walking their dogs, picking up their mail, or mowing their lawns.

This is about more than just finding out whether the neighborhood is cosmetically attractive. When you do this, you're looking for signs of pride of ownership. You want to invest in an area that will be a natural fit for people who take care of themselves and the place where they live. You want a neighborhood that's quiet during working hours, not one where people are drinking beer on the porch in the middle of the day. You want a neighborhood where people are comfortable letting their kids ride bikes up and down the block. You want an area where people don't worry about walking home from the store after dark.

That's not to say that the neighborhood's price point has to be the same as where you and your family live. It's not about class economics. It's about being able to say, "Would I want to live here?"

If your answer is "Hell no!", then obviously it's not the right area for you to invest.

Because here's the thing: attracting good tenants is easiest to do when you're looking for tenants you can relate to. Again, they don't have to make the same income or have the same background as you. But they do have to be people with whom you share common values, especially when it comes to things like responsibility, respect for property, and fulfilling obligations.

My Strategies for Finding Property

As a veteran property investor, I've developed a few prerequisites before I even get in the car to drive around and look at neighborhoods.

1. My preference is to only look in municipalities that have at least 100,000 people. The reason for that is simple: that number makes it likely that I'll have a decently sized rental pool.

2. I look for the area's major employers. Are there universities, manufacturing or some sort of industry hub nearby? Working people typically want to live as close to their place of employment as possible, particularly in an area like Toronto where the traffic is only getting worse by the day. Because my ideal tenant is someone with a job, I want to buy property that offers good proximity to places of employment.

3. Transit systems are set up to take people from low density areas into the higher density areas where you find all the office towers and the jobs that come with them. Here in Toronto, our provincial transit system, the GO Train, extends from the city center all the way down to Niagara Falls. Right now, the number of GO Train stations is increasing, as well as the frequency of travel. When I'm scouting available property, I look at areas where new stations are being built.

4. I look for the neighborhood centers. Where do people go to shop, meet up, and have fun?

5. Another aspect of my ideal tenant is that if they have kids, they care about where those kids go to school. Accordingly, I look for property in areas with proximity not just to schools, but to good schools.

Once I've scouted out those prerequisites, I'll draw a circle of about 10 kilometers around each one. My ideal neighborhood to buy a property is where those circles intersect. That intersection means maximizing the draw of the property I've invested in.

But What About the Great Deals?

I know it can be hard to resist the allure of the impossibly low-priced house, whether it's a foreclosure or just in a deeply blighted area.

There's a website called Homepath.com by Fannie Mae for foreclosed properties—you can see all the foreclosed houses in the United States. I found one property there, a house that was converted into two apartments, for $17,500. I was very tempted. How do you resist a price that low? You can practically put it on a credit card, and with a few basic improvements, the property could cashflow like crazy. What stopped me was the location. The building was in a small community in New Jersey of about 25,000 people. In other words, there was no real demand there, which would mean no appreciation of the overall value.

Great deals feel good in the moment, but again, the real payoff comes from good homes in areas where you could see yourself living today.

That said, if you have an inside line on the next neighborhood to pop off, or you want to take a chance on buying in a blighted neighborhood that could become the next hipster enclave, go for it! (This is the same strategy used by Evelyn, the student property owner I mentioned in Chapter 1.) Just know that you'll have to be prepared either to wait a long time for that investment to pay off or to take whatever tenants you can get. It's great when you can get into an area before everyone else, but you may have to deal with a lower quality of tenant until that area comes into its own.

If you want to get a strong start, look for a good balance between what you pay for the property, and whom you can find to pay you. The fact is that you usually have to pay a reasonable amount if you want to attract reasonable people as tenants. In particular, paying more for a house in an area where land is limited and demand is high means that, when it comes to tenants, you can pick the best of the best and charge accordingly. To me, it's always worth paying a little more (or even a lot more) for a property when it means that I'll start making money right away.

A great example is what happened right at the beginning of the real estate boom in Hamilton, Ontario. A new GO station opened there with transit service to Toronto, and overnight, the price of real estate jumped about 20 percent. A big part of this boom came from people who had been priced out of homes in Toronto, Mississauga, or other places on the outskirts of the Greater Toronto Area—they looked at Hamilton and realized they could buy a 2,400-square-foot home for the same priced they'd paid for an 800-foot condo, and not even have to drive any further. People selling homes in Hamilton were suddenly fielding ten or twelve competing offers at once and selling for well over $100,000 more than their asking price.

Another example comes from my own portfolio. Last year, I bought a bungalow in St. Catharine's for $375,000. I added a bedroom to it and converted the downstairs into a two-bedroom, one-bath apartment. Everything else in that area that's been sold lately with no renovations is going for $495,000 or more. My only regret is that I didn't buy four of those bungalows.

At the end of the day, there's really no secret to being able to make money by investing in real estate. There may be people who claim to have a sixth sense that has made them a fortune—if so, good for them. But honestly, if you just stick to the basics—renting nice homes in nice areas with nice basic improvements to nice tenants—any house can be made to generate cashflow.

Chapter 8

Do I Have the Cash?

I recently sat down with a friend who, after hearing me talk about real estate investment for years, is finally starting to consider it for herself. She's a medical professional, her husband is a police detective, and they have a little side business in bath bombs that has just started to take off. In other words, they have a great income.

That's why I was floored to hear them say, "I don't think we have enough cash to buy a property."

I'm their financial advisor, so I wanted to keep our conversation professional. But it was all I could do to stop myself from shouting, "Are you guys nuts?" Instead, I put on my professional hat to show them all the places where they had money waiting for them and didn't realize it.

Your Money Is Hiding Under Your House

The first and easiest place for anybody to get money is from the equity in their principal residence.

> If you're renting, it's still possible to invest in real estate. However, it's then a question of tapping into your savings as opposed to the equity in your property.

People are always surprised at how much equity they can access from their home. The hard part is showing them the advantage of using that equity to buy assets that create more cashflow.

If you're like a lot of people, you may have it fixed in your mind that before making any major move with your money, you must pay off your mortgage. It's practically a moral imperative in our culture that you have to eliminate your greatest debt before you take on another.

I can understand that perspective, and I certainly don't advocate racking up debt with no plan for paying it back. However, it's important to distinguish between the types of debt you're taking on, and compare the benefit against the cost.

Let's say you have 10 years left to pay off your mortgage. While it's great to eliminate that major expense from your life, waiting until it's gone means that when you're finally ready to invest in a rental property, it's going to be much more expensive—in all likelihood, a difference in the hundreds of thousands of dollars. On the other hand, if you bought the rental property now and got it generating cashflow, in ten years your rental would have appreciated astronomically, to the point where you could likely sell the property, pay off the remaining mortgage, and still have a lot of money left over to enjoy.

I understand the desire to eliminate debt, but it's important to take the long view. Being determined to pay off your mortgage or other debts before investing in property is essentially saying, "I don't want to make more money until I don't have any more big expenses." You're always going to have expenses, whether your mortgage is gone or not. To me, it only makes sense to use the money you have to create an asset that makes even more money that lets you pay off all those debts and start having positive cashflow sooner.

Getting Started

To tap the equity in your home for investment purposes, the first order of business is finding out the current value of your house. If you don't know it offhand, it's very easy to find out. Just visit or call a real estate agent and ask for a list of comparable properties that have sold in the last 90 days. If you want a more formal figure, you can also spend $300 or so to get it appraised by an accredited professional.

If the equity in your home is in the ballpark of the number you need to buy your target property, pull the trigger. The worst that can happen is that if renting your property doesn't work out, you sell it.

In saying that, I'm not advising that you rush to take out a second mortgage without doing your due diligence. As Warren Buffet says, "There are two rules. Rule number one, don't lose money. Rule number two, refer to rule number one." It's important to go into this with eyes wide open and do as much legwork as needed to prove that the property is a viable investment.

For me, a viable investment consists of estimated costs (property purchase and renovations) within a reasonable budget, and a minimum cashflow of $250 to 300.

> Wondering where I get that number? It's pretty simple: if I'm going to be managing the property, I need to be "paying myself" at least $250 to $300 per month.

As we discussed in Chapter 5, cashflow is king. Any business can make big chunks of money from time to time, but stability is what keeps you going. If you don't have that steady, consistent cashflow, your investment will eventually die on the vine.

If tapping into your equity doesn't give you all the capital you need, don't worry. There are other avenues you can go through. One great option is a joint venture partnership, something my firm specializes in.

How a Joint Venture Partnership Works

If real estate investment is the secret sauce for building wealth, joint venture partnerships are the secret ingredient within that sauce. The way we set them up at Magellan Wealth Management, these partnerships offer access to funding and expertise that helps investors buy, improve, and manage their investment property.

You may ask, why wouldn't investors just go to a bank and take out a loan to get the additional funding they need? That's a good question. The answer is that financing policies and the rules governing them are constantly changing. For example, the Canadian government recently set a limit on the number of mortgages banks can provide to any one person—it was their way of putting the brakes on our overheated real estate industry. Joint venture partnerships allow you as the investor to build your portfolio without tapping into your savings or asking a family member or friend for the capital to buy a rental property.

Beyond the funding, however, a significant advantage of our joint venture partnerships is that they make real estate investment as hassle-free as it can be. My team and I scout the neighborhoods, identify good properties, plan and execute the renovations, find and manage the tenants, and take on half the cost of any future problems...the whole nine yards. After fronting the capital, all the investor has to do is collect their share of the profits each month.

A third advantage of joint venture partnership is flexibility in financing. In Canada, you're required by law to put down 20 percent on a house you're financing through a bank. Joint venture partnerships allow you to get creative.

Flexible financing works to your advantage in several ways. The primary advantage, however, is that it expedites the process of accessing capital.

In real estate, time either makes you money or it costs you money. To make the greatest amount of money, you've got to be able to make deals very quickly—sometimes within hours. I've been in situations where an owner is suddenly ready to sell right on the spot, at a bargain price. The only way to make it happen is to produce cash, then and there.

As you probably know from purchasing the home you live in, banks have due diligence processes for granting loans—processes that can take days at a minimum.

In those situations, going to the bank is a good way to lose a great deal. That's why I find it much easier to access capital through a private lender. If you're not able to access sufficient capital through the equity of your home, joint venture partnerships make it possible to pull the trigger on a great opportunity.

> Along with expediting your ability to strike while the iron is hot, investing with a joint venture partnership also allows you to vet your investment partners, ask whatever questions you want, and put everything down in a contract so that you know what you're getting and when you'll get it.

This is exactly what happened last year when I purchased a rental property in St. Catharine's in a joint venture partnership with two investors, who each took on 50 percent of the loan required to buy the property. At the time, I negotiated a price of $375,000 for that house, which included an illegal one-bedroom basement apartment.

If I had gone through a bank on my own, I would have had to put down $75,000 plus closing costs and come up with the capital to execute the needed renovations. Not to mention the bank would have had an issue with the illegal apartment.

Instead, each investor loaned me $185,000 via a private mortgage set up in their respective RRSP accounts. I put in $30,000 of my own for renovations to make the apartment a two-bedroom legal dwelling, which instantly forced the appreciation of the house. Once I got the house generating cashflow, I began paying back my investors at a rate of 8% per year. When the time is right, I will refinance the mortgage to pay off my investors completely.

The house is now valued at $495,000, an increase of $120,000. If any of us had waited ten years or so to pay off our mortgage before trying to purchase that house, it would probably be worth $800,000—nearly double what it costs now. Instead of watching our investment gain roughly $90,000 in value, we would have had to put down almost double that amount to buy at twice the cost.

You Don't Need as Much Money as You Think You Need

The most common objection I hear from people about real estate investment is that they assume they need a lot of money to do it. That is not the case at all. In fact, I've had people borrow from a line of credit to lend to me—a risky move on the face of it, but they saw that the security that I provided was enough to decrease their risk.

A few years ago, I began advising a woman named Jen, who had retired from UPS without much of a pension. She was facing a future of living from paycheque to paycheque—no vacations, no big gifts to her family, nothing extravagant. However, she had one significant asset—her house was paid off.

Jen had looked into investing in mutual funds, but she found it hard to understand, and the rate of return didn't offer what she was looking for. When I explained how real estate investment could give her the stability of a consistent rate of return, she was intrigued. However, she had a hard time believing that she could enter the real estate market with the meager savings she had to her name. I explained that by unlocking the value trapped in the value of her house, she could deploy that significant asset in a way that would give her a stable income in retirement.

Jen was still a little skeptical—to her, it all sounded too good to be true. She was also very clear that she didn't want a new job as a landlord. Therefore, I proposed that she join Magellan Wealth Management as a joint venture partner. She could put a line of credit on her house and use it to lend my firm a mortgage. Her only cost would be the monthly interest on the line of credit. In turn, we would pay her 8 percent for the money she'd lent, far more stable than the return a mutual fund would give her.

With the money she lent my firm, I was able to make a cash offer for a property and secured a much lower price than if we'd taken a traditional financing route. The seller was happy to lower their asking price if it meant getting all their money up front, instead of waiting for it to be financed. Jen was happy because she made 8 percent on the equity that had formerly been trapped in the value of her home. She saw that it didn't need an enormous amount of money or time for her investment to pay off. Instead of letting all that money just sit there, she could put it to work for her.

She became even happier as, over the six-month term of the mortgage she lent to my firm, her rate of return was 37 percent (This is the power of leverage at work). Ask anyone in financial planning, and they'll tell that you a rate of return that high is practically unheard of in a mutual fund portfolio, certainly not on any consistent basis. That's another advantage with lending privately—fluctuations in the market don't affect your rate of return.

> It's true that the potential downside of private lending is that it's typically not liquid. You can't simply walk back into the bank, sell your position and get your money back. However, engaging a real estate investment consultant with a wide network means that if you should need to take your money out of an investment, you can usually find someone else to take over your position as the lender in that mortgage.

But it wasn't until Magellan Wealth Management cut her a check for $25,000 on top of what she'd lent us that Jen realized what kind of impact that change really had. With the return on just one property, she had her entire income for the year. Real estate investment completely changed her prospects for retirement.

Stop Getting in the Way of Your Dream

You can't take advantage of yesterday's opportunities today. The best opportunity you have is always the one in front of you right now. Yes, there will be opportunities down the road, but they will never be as good as they are today.

As the saying goes, the definition of insanity is doing the same thing over and over again and expecting a different outcome. So, if you want to make a difference in your finances, you have to take different actions from what you're accustomed to. Even a small change is worth making—it gets you farther forward than you were before. If you don't think you can handle a real estate investment, but you want to be in it, all it takes is finding someone who knows what they're doing.

Everyone has a dream for what they want their money to accomplish for them. But that dream doesn't come true on its own. You have to take steps today to make it happen.

FREE READER RESOURCES

Sometimes it's useful to clear down your debt. I wrote a Bonus chapter for this book with a simple strategy any investor can use to reduce their leverage by paying off their mortgage in half the time.

You can download it FREE at

www.PropertyProfitsToolbox.com

Conclusion

By now, you've seen that real estate investment offers the potential to create significant change in both your lifestyle today and your plans for the future. Better still, getting started is much simpler than you probably imagined it could be. The only question left in your mind at this point is wondering how successful you personally can be.

There are two kinds of people who are most successful in real estate investment.

On the one hand, there are the people who recognize the "business in a box" nature of real estate and who are game for the challenge of being a business owner. If you have an entrepreneurial nature, you're perfectly positioned to scout properties, negotiate for them, fix them up and manage them yourself.

On the other hand, there are the investors who want to be as uninvolved as possible. They want to use the funds they've saved up, put it into a property where it will grow quickly, and watch for their cheques to arrive in the mail.

Needless to say, this is the easier route...and there's no shame in taking it! Unless you're someone who gets a kick out of doing deals, swinging a hammer, or troubleshooting tenant issues, the last thing you want is a second job on your hands, especially in retirement.

If you prefer the idea of sitting back and letting your money do all the work for you, the joint venture partnership is for you. And by working with an experienced real estate investment consultant, you can start your investment journey with confidence.

It's important to choose a real estate investment consultant whose preferred exit strategy and approach to real estate investment matches your own. Personally, I specialize in buying decent single-family homes, maximizing the investment with cost-effective renovations, and cutting my investors cheques that put a smile on their faces every month.

Here's how the joint venture partnership works:

- First, my team sits down to talk with you about your goals. What do you want your money to accomplish for you, both in the short-term and in the long-term? How involved do you want to be in the "life" of your investment? What kind of capital are you able to access? Once we assess your needs and preferences, we present the options for investment that are best for building your individual portfolio.
- We scout the best neighborhoods and identify a property that fits your needs.
- We negotiate the sale and navigate through the process of inspection and other conditions.
- We execute a co-ownership agreement that details what each of the partners can expect.

- We find the contractors needed to execute the project.
- We create drawings for renovation and conversion, and obtain the necessary permits.
- We coordinate with your mortgage broker of choice, or offer the option of doing it in-house.
- We manage the renovation process, interview and select tenants, troubleshoot any issues that come up during the life of the property, and monitor the home/neighborhood's value for future opportunities.
- Once tenants move in, we assume 50 percent of all risks, including any new construction costs.

In short, we do the work to make sure that your property makes money. It's just like investing in mutual funds, without all the mystery and market volatility.

…Oh, and with a much better rate of return.

The Time Is Now

People will tell you there's only one way to make your money work for you. You can either listen to them and keep living the way you always have—sweating out the monthly bills, crossing your fingers that your retirement account will be enough to fund your lifestyle when you stop working—or you can be the one to show them what's really possible when you step outside the box, take control of your finances, and do something that makes sense to you.

It's worth thinking over. But not for too long. The true wealth component in real estate is time. It's not just having the asset, but it's the length of time that you have it, that really builds your wealth.

To put it another way, time is not your friend. The cost of entry will only go up the longer you wait.

Are You Ready for the Next Step?

If you're sick of financial anxiety and ready for change, now is the moment to take action. Visit

www.LetsTalkRealEstate.Today

to choose a date for your free consultation with our team of property investment experts. We look forward to helping you take the first steps in creating the lifestyle you've been dreaming about.

CPSIA information can be obtained
at www.ICGtesting.com
Printed in the USA
LVHW030431230420
653992LV00001B/1